LIVING THROUGH

THE GALE

SKIPPER'S LIBRARY

LIVING THROUGH

THE GALE

BEING PREPARED FOR HEAVY WEATHER

TOM CUNLIFFE

FERNHURST
BOOKS

Published in 2023 by Fernhurst Books Limited.
The Windmill, Mill Lane, Harbury, Leamington Spa, Warwickshire. CV33 9HP, UK
Tel: +44 (0) 1926 337488 | www.fernhurstbooks.com

A catalogue record for this book is available from the British Library
ISBN: 9781912621637

Front & back cover photographs © Tom Cunliffe
Other photo credits, see Page 144

Designed by Daniel Stephen
Printed in India by Replika Press Pvt. Ltd.

CONTENTS

TOM CUNLIFFE

Tom Cunliffe is Britain's leading sailing writer. A worldwide authority on cruising instruction and an expert on traditional sailing craft, he learnt his sextant skills during numerous ocean passages, many in simple boats without engines or electronics, voyaging from Brazil to Greenland and from the Caribbean to Russia. He is a consultant for US Sailing and author of numerous maritime textbooks.

Tom's nautical career has seen him serve as mate on a merchant ship, captain on gentleman's yachts and skipper of racing craft. He has owned a series of traditional gaff-rigged vessels that have taken him and his family on countless adventures from tropical rainforests to frozen fjords, but he now sails a modern classic 44-foot cutter which he keeps in Scandinavia.

Tom has been a Yachtmaster Examiner since 1978 and has a gift for sharing his knowledge with good humour and an endless supply of tales of the sea.

He has monthly columns in *Sailing Today*, *Classic Boat*, *Yachting World* and *SAIL* (US) magazines. He wrote and presented the BBC TV series *The Boats That Built Britain* and the popular *Boatyard* series. His YouTube channel (search 'Tom Cunliffe Yachts and Yarns') has a global audience.

Scan to visit Tom's YouTube channel

During the Covid lockdown he set up an online club for sailors worldwide. This has proved very popular with a monthly Zoom Q&A forum, articles and videos by Tom, an audiobook and book recommendations. All for just £15 a year. To join go to: www.tomcunliffe.com where you will also find information about his various lectures, etc.

Scan to visit Tom's website

Tom has written 7 other books for Fernhurst Books:

200 Skipper's Tips
Boat Handling Under Sail & Power
Celestial Navigation
Coastal & Offshore Navigation
Expert Sailing Skills
Inshore Navigation
Sailing, Yachts & Yarns

INTRODUCTION

Nobody but the most extreme enthusiast wants to be at sea in heavy weather, but it's out there nonetheless. Anyone planning on crossing an ocean must be ready to meet it if it comes, as well it may. Inshore and continental-shelf sailors can still be caught out despite today's remarkable weather forecasting. The object of this slim, quickly absorbed volume is to give all sailors, whatever their passage-making aspirations, a sound brief so that whether they find themselves at the wrong end of a force-six blow along the coast, or confronting serious waves far out at sea, they are fully aware of their options for taking it in their stride.

Every sailor is fascinated by the subject of heavy weather. There are probably more strongly held opinions about how to cope with it than any other question related to seafaring, but if you try to define it you soon discover that, like happiness, hard going is different things to different people. An experienced crew in a 50-foot cutter sailing on a broad reach in 25 knots of wind ought to be thoroughly enjoying themselves. In the same conditions, a family group who have been working to windward for 24 hours in a 20-foot bilge keeler could well be near snapping point.

Heavy weather could be characterised as any combination of wind and sea of sufficient severity to cause the crew of a particular boat to consider altering their plans. But weather at sea is capable of worsening far beyond that marginal situation, and sooner or later any boat may meet circumstances in which she can do little more than drift helplessly into mortal danger. The art of skippering is to handle yourself, your crew and your boat so that you steer clear of that final truth for a whole lifetime. The list of essential equipment to achieve this is short. It consists of a well-found yacht, a sound knowledge of the options available and a positive, self-reliant approach.

The strong message throughout this book is one of self-help. It's about making the most of your own resources to keep clear of trouble if you can, and dealing with it if you can't. For all these fine intentions, however, the sea very occasionally brings our own efforts to nothing, so the chapters on Emergencies, The Liferaft and Outside Assistance consider the sort of situation that can arise one day for any of us who stay out there long enough. However carefully we prepare, there always remains the possibility that the weather and other circumstances will combine against us and leave us at the end of our tether. These chapters discuss how to approach the question of outside assistance, when it may realistically be needed and how to handle oneself in connection with it.

Sailing in heavy weather is an inevitable part of life on the water. It can be a nightmare, or it may provide that spice of real action which many sailors secretly – or not so secretly – desire. Coming through a blow undamaged and without fuss pulls a crew together. They'll talk about it years later and the satisfaction they feel with their boat and one another is something special. The means of achieving this result are latent in all of us. The following pages will help you to identify and draw on them at sea when the wind blows hard.

As an afterthought, in these times of inclusivity I have endeavoured throughout the book to avoid personal pronouns implying gender. Without apology, however, I have maintained the ancient tradition of the sea by referring to ships and boats as 'she'. No offence is intended or implied.

Tom Cunliffe
March 2023

1

WIND & WAVE

WIND

Wind is what sailing is all about. Wind powers the rig which drives the boat along; wind heels the boat over; wind direction decides whether we beat or sail free; wind strength and direction are the weather predictions in which we are most interested. Wind also stirs up the surface of the sea and makes waves, and in the last analysis it is waves which are most likely to spoil our day.

THE BEAUFORT SCALE IN PERSPECTIVE

If you listen to broadside folk ballads of the eighteenth century you will hear some strange weather reports. We are advised that when General Wolfe's men set sail, 'the wind it blew a pleasant gale'. This sort of muddy concept of weather conditions became obsolete when Admiral Beaufort produced his famous scale of wind forces.

Originally designed for use in Royal Navy ships it related wind speed to the sails a standard frigate or ship of the line would choose to set, all things being equal. His wind forces ran from 0-12 and so successful were his efforts that to this day many maritime nations still refer to wind strength on the Beaufort Scale.

The table to the right is a yachtsman's Beaufort Scale. The wind and sea states are related to three typical modern yachts. One is a 22-foot cruising sloop with twin bilge keels. She is roomy, but not very powerful; she has an inboard diesel engine. The second is a typical 36-foot cruiser with a fin keel and a spade rudder. She will have a flat amidships section and will perform well in flat water. Going upwind in a seaway she may well slam. The last is a serious deep-water cruising yacht, designed and built to take rough weather in her stride. For convenience, each is assumed to have a good suit of sails, with a three-slab reefing mainsail and a roller genoa. The shortcomings of the reefed genoa are shown in the table and some alternatives are offered. These are available to any boat, but are not usually 'plug and play'. They may require some modifications to a standard vessel. All the boats are sailing to windward in open water. Below the heavy line each will experience considerable problems and, while all is not lost, progress to windward may prove ineffective without power assistance. Ultimately, it becomes impossible.

Wind Force	Wind Speed		Description
	Metres per second – mps	Knots	
0	<0.5	<1	Calm
1	0.5-1.5	1-3	Light Air
2	1.6-3.3	4-6	Light Breeze
3	3.4-5.4	7-10	Gentle Breeze
4	5.5-7.9	11-16	Moderate Breeze
5	8.0-10.7	17-21	Fresh Breeze
6	10.8-13.8	22-27	Strong Breeze
7	13.9-17.1	28-33	Near Gale
8	17.2-20.7	34-40	Gale
9	20.8-24.4	41-47	Severe Gale
10	24.5-27.0	48-55	Storm
11	28.0-32.0	56-63	Violent Storm
12	>32.0	>64	Hurricane

Probable Wave Height		Typical cruising boats – Wind Forward of the Beam		
Min Feet (metres)	Max Feet (metres)	22' Bilge Keeler	36' Fin & Spade-Profile Cruiser	50' Heavy Displacement Cruiser
0	0	Motoring	Motoring	Motoring
0	0	Motoring	Motoring	Motoring
0	0.75 (0.2)	Genoa & full main	Genoa & full main	Genoa & full main
1 (0.3)	3 (1)	Genoa & full main	Genoa & full main	Genoa & full main
3 (1)	4 (1.5)	1 reef in main, genoa reefed	1 reef in main, full genoa	Genoa & full main
4 (1.5)	8 (2.5)	2 reefs in main, more rolls in genoa	1 reef in main, 4 rolls in genoa	1 reef in main, some boats 2 rolls in genoa
8 (2.5)	11 (3.5)	3 reefs in main, genoa at minimum with seriously reduced performance	2 (3) reefs in main, further rolls in genoa	1 reef in main, 4 rolls in genoa
11 (3.5)	16 (5)	3 reefs in main, motor?	3 reefs in main, genoa no longer viable; deploy storm jib or motor-sail	2 reefs in main, genoa rolled to minimum viable size or specialised blade headsail
16 (5)	21 (6.5)	3 reefs in main, motor?? Very little progress to windward	3 reefs in main or trysail, storm jib if available; otherwise motor-sail	3 reefs in main, blade if appropriate or storm jib
21 (6.5)	27 (8)	Survival conditions	Trysail / storm jib / motor; very heavy going	Trysail, storm jib
27 (8)	35 (10)		Upwind progress barely possible; some boats now in survival mode	Motor assistance
35 (10)	45 (13)		Survival conditions	Survival conditions
48 (14)	Very high			

Moving on in time from the days when Nelson's captains were deciding whether or not to double-reef their topsails, more recent versions of the scale describe the sea conditions found in typical wind strengths. These are surprisingly useful and, until masthead anemometers became standard equipment for seagoing yachts, knowing that in force 7, foam becomes organised into long streaks behind wave crests was a big help.

Nowadays, wind force is accurately quantified by onboard instruments and internet weather sites, most giving predictions in knots or metres per second. In a sense, however, nothing has changed. Regardless of what the numbers are on the dial, the main concern of a yacht skipper is about the question of shortening sail rather than whether the apparent wind is blowing at 17 knots or 8mps.

WIND PRESSURE

As wind speed increases, the pressure exerted by the flowing air rises at a dramatic rate. At 15 knots (force 4), it is 0.8 pounds per square foot. At 30 knots (force 7) it has quadrupled to 3.1 pounds per square foot, and by the time the heady figure of 60 knots comes along in a full hurricane-force blow, we are up to around 12.3 pounds.

The units of measurement are unimportant in practice, so if you think in kilograms and square metres with wind strength defined in metres per second, it matters not. In this context at least, it's the proportions that count and they don't change.

A ghastly shock awaits the inexperienced mariner who is under the impression that force 8 is twice as windy as force 4. Five times as bad is nearer the mark and, of course, that's only the wind. The real enemy is the sea.

GUSTS

Forecast wind strengths were traditionally given as mean wind speeds. Some still are, but wind predictions published on the internet will typically give a mean wind and what is described as a 'gust speed'. Very often, the gust will be double the mean, leaving the user to make the judgement call while covering the forecasters against contingencies.

The fact is that a strong breeze officially described as being force 6 (22-27 knots) may, in fact, vary from 20 knots in the lulls to some evil gusts blasting up to 30. Twenty knots is force 5 on the Beaufort Scale, comfortably within the windward capacity of a small cruiser. Thirty knots is well into force 7, which is double the real wind force, and is

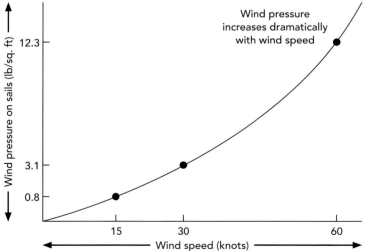

Wind pressure increases dramatically with wind speed

Wind pressure increases dramatically with wind speed

quite capable of giving such a boat a very unpleasant afternoon.

Recognising this, forecasts are now usually given with a mean wind and a gust speed.

In open water, different types of air mass will lead to more or less gusty conditions. The unstable polar maritime air that comes swishing down behind a cold front in temperate latitudes is high on the gustiness list whereas a stable 'tropical maritime' south-westerly breeze at 50° North is likely to be a lot steadier.

SQUALLS

A squall is a local disturbance in the airstream which, in one form or another, produces conditions more violent than those currently being experienced.

You can usually see a squall coming because its presence is given away by a cloud effect. Squall clouds come in various shapes and sizes and will be discussed in Chapter 4. For now it is enough to understand that a bad squall can turn fifteen minutes of a fresh, windy day into a temporary horror show.

LOCAL EFFECTS ON A STEADY WIND

A given surface wind blows more strongly over the sea than it does over land because water offers less frictional resistance to its passing. The presence of land also tends to break up the steady flow of air. These two factors mean that close to leeward of a coastline there is often a zone where the wind is lighter than it is offshore. However, certain types of land mass can cause accelerated wind speeds or eccentric wind directions.

Air funnelling down a valley to windward will frequently create a local increase in wind speed, while immediately to windward of a high land mass or a steep cliff there may be a zone of light or turbulent wind.

You can usually see a squall coming

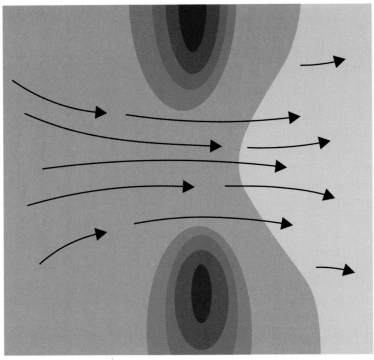

Air blowing through a gap in the hills on a nearby coast will often cause a local increase in wind speed over the sea to leeward

If the high land is the right shape, the wind may well be accelerated down the lee side, causing considerably increased gusting. In locations where particularly steep mountains coincide with narrow sea leads, such as the fjords of western Norway, some fearsome conditions of this type may be experienced. The Norwegians call this a 'falling wind'; as the author discovered to his cost. Such terrible winds have a measurable downward component, and are no fun at all.

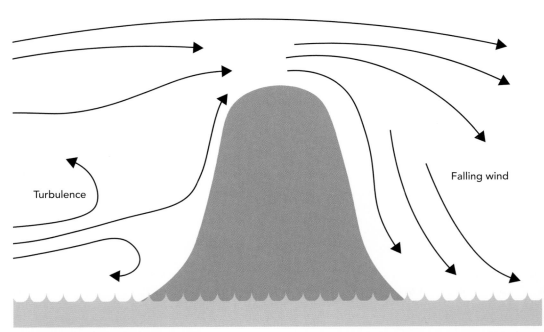

Turbulence

Falling wind

High land can have dramatic effects on local wind conditions with turbulence to windward and occasional 'falling winds' to leeward

So don't assume you'll get a lee from land to weather of you. It may help the sea state, but its effect on the wind will be less predictable.

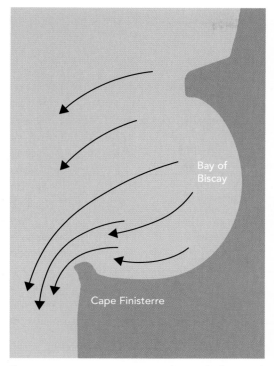 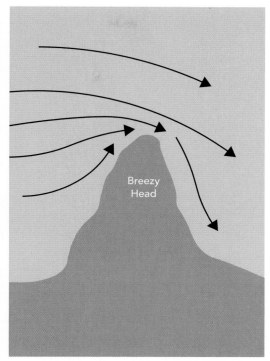

Breezy corners may occur at the end of a continental landmass such as Cape Finisterre (left) or on a projecting headland (right)

TRUE & APPARENT WIND

An understanding of the difference between true and apparent wind is of particular importance in bad weather. True wind is the airstream experienced passively by a boat that is stationary. Once that boat starts moving through the water she moves through the air as well, and this has a direct effect on the wind blowing across her deck.

If a boat motors at six knots in still air, she receives a six-knot headwind. This is obviously apparent wind. Conversely if she motors downwind at six knots in a six-knot breeze, she would feel no wind at all: an apparent lack of wind. If she now turns and motors dead to windward at six knots in the same six-knot breeze, the wind at her

masthead transducer will appear to blow at 12 knots.

There is, therefore, a 12-knot difference in the wind the boat actually experiences (the apparent wind) if she is travelling upwind or downwind.

When the true wind is averaging 28 knots (the bottom end of force 7) a boat running before it at six knots will be enjoying a fine sailing breeze of 22 knots (force 5 or 6). Close-hauled upwind, her apparent wind will increase to something approaching force 8, a whole gale. The pressure of the wind on a given sail area will double, and instead of running comfortably with the sea the boat will have to smash her way through every wave. She is in an entirely different world.

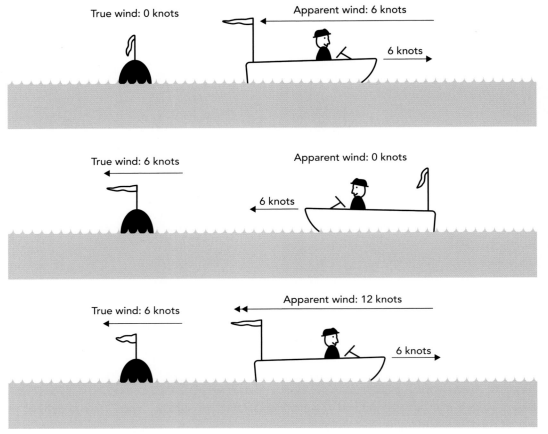

True wind: 0 knots

Apparent wind: 6 knots

6 knots

True wind: 6 knots

Apparent wind: 0 knots

6 knots

True wind: 6 knots

Apparent wind: 12 knots

6 knots

Apparent wind is a combination of the true wind speed and the boat's speed; both the strength and direction of the apparent wind are affected

WAVES

At sea in hard weather the three primary sources of danger are wind, sea state and poor visibility. Unless it rises to extremes, wind alone is rarely a problem for a well-found vessel. A good navigator, whether electronically assisted or not, can handle a lack of visibility effectively. Waves, however, are a different story.

Waves shake and wring a boat like a terrier with a rat, and sometimes they explode against her like a sledgehammer. They test her sternly every time she makes a passage and should she be found wanting in any of her many departments, we have problems.

Waves cause skipper and crew to get wet and, in consequence, cold. They make many of us seasick and can, by this means, reduce a capable hand to a human liability for the duration of a rough passage. Even if we are not sick, waves still make the yacht jump about like a crazy thing, rendering such niceties as cooking and navigation near-impossible sophistications.

Waves can also overwhelm us, roll us over and, in the end, drown us.

We need to give them some serious thought.

THEORETICAL WAVES IN DEEP WATER

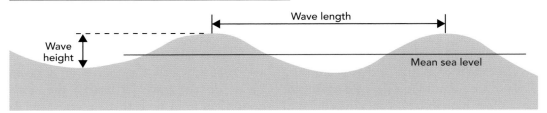

Wave length

Wave height

Mean sea level

In theory, waves in deep, open water should assume a regular sine-wave profile; in practice the effects of wind and tide cause considerable variation

When a breeze blows across mirror-calm water it causes the formation of perfectly shaped waves an even distance apart. At lower wind speeds these waves approximate to the regular shape of a sine wave (see diagram). The distance between the wave crests is called the **wavelength** and, if this is long enough, the waves will have a gentle enough gradient to cause no trouble to a small boat.

As wind velocities increase towards gale and storm force, wave shape tends to change, becoming steeper until finally the wave can no longer support itself and the strength of the wind blowing across the top helps it to break.

Wave height is measured from trough to crest (see diagram). If wave development is unimpeded, the height of the waves caused by a steady wind in open water will go on increasing until they achieve the 'probable wave height' for that strength of wind (see the Beaufort Scale on pages 10-11).

Wave height depends upon **fetch**, which is the distance that the wind has blown uninterrupted over open water. For example, the probable wave height developed in theory by a force 8 wind is given as around 5.5 metres, but with a fetch of even 50 miles it is unlikely to exceed three metres.

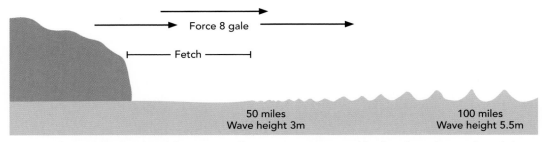

Force 8 gale

Fetch

50 miles
Wave height 3m

100 miles
Wave height 5.5m

In a steady wind the height of the waves will increase as you travel further from the windward shore; this distance is known as the fetch

The **length of time** the wind has been blowing is also a factor in wave size. It takes many hours to build up to the theoretical mean wave height for a given wind force. So in waters not open to the wide ocean it is unusual for these heights to be achieved during the average summer blow.

Wave speeds generally end up as about 60 percent of the mean wind speed if it blows long enough for things to settle down to any degree of regularity.

The effect of all this is that a breaking wave in a moderate force 8 gale is likely to be 18 feet high (5.5m) with a maximum of 25 feet (7.5m), steep-sided and travelling at up to 30 knots or so. Not a pretty proposition, even though it is only the crest that is breaking.

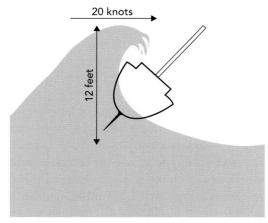

20 knots

12 feet

Beam-on to a breaking wave in a gale

WAVES IN PRACTICE

An ideal series of waves never normally appears at sea. This is because the wind varies, not only in strength, but also in direction. In any case, there is nearly always an old sea left over or another one coming from somewhere else, or both, or worse, such as when tide or current runs contrary to the flowing air.

In real life, because of variations in wind velocity, all the waves in a given series do not travel at exactly the same speed, so from time to time one catches up with another. When this happens the two can combine to produce a wave half as big again as the regular wave height being experienced. These are not the 'freak waves' beloved of the media. They are predictable and appear in wave height tables as 'probable maximum wave height' (see Beaufort Scale on pages 10-11).

WINDSHIFTS

The vast majority of gales and good solid blows will, at some stage of their lives, give their victims the benefit of a substantial windshift.

I have waited eagerly for many a cold front to mark the beginning of the end of a gale out in the North Atlantic, only to discover that as the scudding cloud breaks up and the wind veers to the northwest the sea gets a whole lot worse before it gets any better.

It stands to reason that if you have an established army of contented 25-foot seas marching uniformly out of the west and you suddenly remove their motive force to replace it with a new one from a different direction, the waves are going to get confused. Unfortunately, when they are subjected to this indignity, they don't all suddenly execute a right wheel and stride away before the new wind. Instead, they maintain their progress towards the east while a new bunch begins marching over the top of them. The results are evil. Mostly the combatants sidle around one another with less fuss than one might expect, but when two big ones meet in confrontation they either rear up in a tower of breaking water and collapse in chaos on the spot, or they get together in a sort of lethal truce and go thundering away like a salt-water avalanche, very dangerously if you happen to be in the way.

The sea can get very confused with wind from different directions

THE 'SMOOTH'

Every so often the wave pattern (or lack of it) in a rough sea produces a short period when an area of water is relatively calm. These events are known as 'smooths'.

If you plan on carrying out a manoeuvre such as tacking or gybing it is well worth waiting for a smooth. A smooth may last half a minute or more, or it may be merely a gap of a few seconds before the next big wave arrives. You may never get one, but if there is a smooth coming your way it is a lot easier to wait for it than to tack your ship in the face of a series of steep waves.

Try to identify a smooth to carry out a manoeuvre

TIDE & CURRENT

If you take a normal wave pattern and impose a weather-going current upon it, the seas will heap up in what can appear to be personal spite. The waves become shorter and steeper and break much more readily in consequence. In heavy conditions a bad sea may become dangerous as the tide turns to windward.

A nasty sea created by wind against tide

On the ocean you can often observe when you have run into an adverse current by looking at the sea, in even moderate weather. Telltale streaks of foam running down the backs of the waves as the current carries them to windward is the sign to look for.

In tidal waters the steepening effect on the waves as wind-with-tide changes through slack water to wind-against-tide is dramatic. Indeed, you can judge the turn on the tide on a windy day more accurately by observation than by referring to the tide tables. In the mid-English Channel, for example, where tides can run at three knots or more out of sight of land, the turn of the tide is obvious in bad weather by virtue of the change in sea state.

It's worth remembering that a turning tide can also have a dramatic effect on apparent wind. If the wind is blowing in the same directional vector as the tide, a three-knot stream reversing makes a 6-knot difference to wind blowing across the water, transforming a 24-knot force 6 into a force 7 near gale.

Wind against tide: the same wind strength blowing with the tide (left) and against the tide (right)

RACES & RIPS

In some places the nature of the seabed or the shape of a headland will cause the formation of **tide-induced waves**.

An uneven bottom can incite the running tide to upwell in whirlpools or stopper waves just as individual bottom variations do in a white-water river.

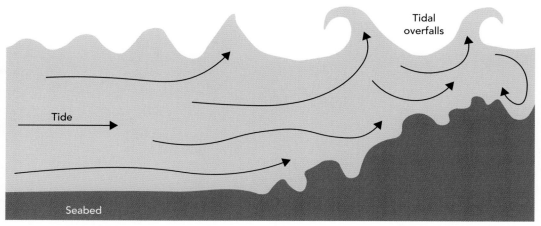

A tidal stream upwelling over a rocky seabed will often create a patch of angry, turbulent water

Tidal overfalls in the Solent

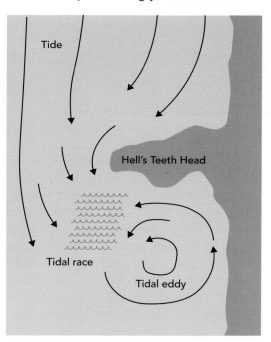

Certain headlands and passages produce rough water, regardless of wind conditions. In the illustration the eddy running westward along the south side of the headland meets the main stream in a mass of broken water that you enter at your peril.

An innocent-looking headland may conspire with the tide to create a race of blood-curdling ferocity; this is exactly what happens at places like Portland: extremely nasty on a calm day, death-traps in heavy weather

A notorious example of this is found at Portland Bill in the English Channel. Another one that can be equally nasty is the Raz de Barfleur on the French side. These places are always far worse at spring tides than at neaps, and if you spice things up with an onshore gale as well, the combination can be literally lethal.

Sail into a bad tide-race on such a day and you may join the ghostly fleets of those who did not emerge to tell the tale.

Portland Bill with the notorious overfalls in the distance

It doesn't always take a gale to whip things up either. I will never forget sailing into what should have been a modest tide rip off St Alban's Head – also in the English Channel. The experience came soon after I'd come through two full-blown autumn storms in the North Atlantic. St Alban's doesn't have a particularly ugly reputation, and the weather was positively benign, but the place was on top form that day with what could only be described as 'wall-to-wall breakers'. My boat was spun round and round. Steering was impossible. We gybed, came aback, square waves leapt aboard and filled the cockpit as we were set onwards by the roaring tide.

Ten minutes later, the same tide spat us out into calm water once more. We survived, shaken, but mercifully without damage. It's not an experience I'd care to repeat. Had we not seen what was coming in time, battened down and clipped on we would have been swamped and could well have had someone thrown overboard. I realised later that I'd been caught out by a big swell left over from a mid-Atlantic storm. This came sweeping in against the spring tide which I'd caught in full spate. Sometimes, it pays to think beyond the next forecast.

Treat tide races with great care!

SHALLOW WATER EFFECTS

Theoretical mean and maximum wave heights hold good only so long as the sea is deep enough to support them. Here is what happens when a series of waves enters shoaling water.

In a fresh to strong breeze the wave condition on a lee shore, even if fully formed, is unaffected until the water shoals to about 40 metres. From this point on the waves begin to ease a little, growing shorter and somewhat smaller. As the bottom comes closer, the waves gradually become shorter still and take on a steeper shape. They are unwilling to break, however, until the depth has shoaled to between one and a half and two times the height of the wave, after which they cannot survive and break heavily.

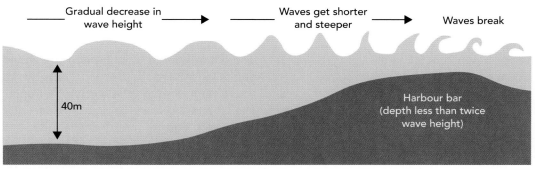

Gradual decrease in wave height → Waves get shorter and steeper → Waves break

40m

Harbour bar (depth less than twice wave height)

In shoaling water the waves get shorter and steeper, and will often break over the harbour bar

If you are sailing anywhere near a lee shore in a blow you need to be aware of how the waves will react, particularly if you have to cross the bar of a river. Add an ebbing tide to seas which are approaching their natural breaking point and you have another situation not to be tolerated.

Countless well-found vessels have completed their voyage only to be dumped terminally on the harbour bar at their destination – very likely by the first breaker of the falling tide. There has to be a first. Always bear in mind, if in doubt, that it may be waiting just for you.

Notorious estuary bar in north Cornwall on a calm day; when it's rough, it lives up to it's name: Doom Bar

The bar at Salcombe harbour in southwest England is another famous for dangerous seas on the ebb in an onshore gale.

Many harbour mouths on the Atlantic coast of Portugal can become untenable when a big swell is running in from the ocean. Sailing five miles offshore you notice nothing untoward, but as you approach the breakwaters, you realise that a huge swell is developing, getting steeper and steeper until you almost literally surf in through the entrance, grateful to have been spared. In hard weather such places are not to be countenanced. Read the pilot book and take notice of what it says. For further confirmation of how dangerous this sort of thing can be, Google 'Nazaré surf YouTube' and marvel at what you see.

Off-lying banks are also subject to these effects. Sometimes they are marked as dangerous on the chart ('breaks in westerly gales' or 'breaks heavily'), but not always. If you are unsure, consult your pilot book but be ever wary in gale conditions, particularly if the tide is pouring into the eye of the wind.

CLIFFS & BREAKWATERS

When a sea runs squarely up to a wall it bounces straight back out again like a squash ball. It matters not whether the wall was put there by God as a cliff face or by man in the form of a harbour wall.

In heavy weather the effects of this can be grim, so you should anticipate some severe wave activity if you find you are approaching a harbour with a breakwater that forms a lee shore with sea breaking against it.

Such a refuge would be a dubious option anyway, but waves bouncing back and running into one another add directly to each other's height and break with the ferocity of a tide rip in full cry. A small vessel caught in a sea like this is liable to lose control of her steering and she would be lucky indeed if the wind saw fit to squirt her in through the harbour entrance. The alternatives are to scrape clear with a bruised ego or be overwhelmed and wrecked.

The conditions such situations produce in a whole gale need to be experienced to be believed. Better by far to go elsewhere or remain offshore where the big seas roll by more benevolently. Except in the most extreme circumstances, the sea alone is rarely the ultimate enemy. Real danger occurs at the interface between sea and land.

When waves meet the land, the effects can be grim

2

FIT FOR SEA: THE BOAT

The sea is no respecter of half measures. A boat and everything to do with her must be made as right as can be before she is taken offshore. In the halcyon days when proverbs were coined, the mariner was encouraged not to spoil his ship 'for a ha'p'orth of tar'. Put into the perspective of the twenty-first century it would be more realistic to consider the ruinous consequences of failing to replace a few hundred pounds-worth of tired gear.

There is no short cut. You just have to pay. Even if you do all your own work, you still have to buy materials, so it's 'groan you may, but go you must' when it comes to stumping up for your boat maintenance. There is no worse feeling for a sailor than looking aloft at a vital shackle that should by rights have been replaced, and hoping it holds. Especially when lives may depend on it.

You can get away with shoddy gear for months of sunshine yachting, but the first gale-force squall that catches you offshore has an uncanny way of revealing all.

A modern yacht can be divided into four main parts for the purposes of serious preparation for sea: the hull, the rig, the engine and the rest. We'll look at them one by one.

THE HULL

It goes without saying that so long as the hull is afloat the crew are in with a chance, so the watertight integrity of the hull must be the prime objective when listing priorities.

In the case of all but the very lightest designs, fibreglass hulls stay pretty watertight so long as they do not run into anything. Bolt-on keels have been known to part company with the hull which is of course catastrophic, but such events are mercifully rare. Hulls built of ferrocement, steel and monocoque composite are also tight by definition. A traditional wooden hull is as good as its original construction and subsequent lifelong maintenance. Given conscientious attention, it may well be better than adequate. It is rare for a hull to let itself down. More often it is the official holes in it which allow water in when they shouldn't.

If the hull is watertight, it will keep the crew above water when all seems lost

Seacocks, including those for cockpit drains, must be regularly serviced. They, their associated skin fittings and hoses must be regularly checked.

Stern glands should be in perfect order. Sinking because a stuffing box fails or the bellows on a deep-sea seal perish and rupture is entirely avoidable.

Hatches have got to be burst proof. I have seen production forehatches I could kick my boot through, secured by catches that I would not put on a washroom door. Make sure yours are up to the job.

Make sure your forehatch is made of burst-proof material, and fitted with strong catches

Companionway washboards need to have a lock-in facility, and the sliding hatch itself must be capable of being secured and opened from both above and below decks.

Companionway washboards must be solid, and capable of being locked and unlocked from outside and inside

A substantial bridge deck or companionway sill should separate the cockpit from the main entrance to the accommodation.

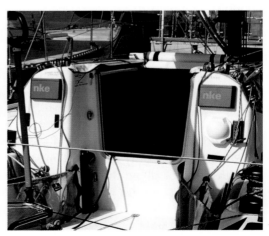

A substantial companionway sill should separate the cockpit from the main entrance to the accommodation

This sill you would hardly trip over and it certainly wouldn't stop much water

Cockpit locker lids provide wonderful access for the sea if the boat is thrown over and they're not fastened down. A modern wide-sterned yacht has cavernous lockers which can take in enough water to do a lot of harm.

If a locker lid falls open during a knockdown the sea will pour in and could easily flood the boat

When a boat is knocked down it is generally the windows on the leeward side which are damaged as the boat slams into the solid water in the trough of the wave. Contrary to what you might expect, this is like being dropped onto a concrete parking lot – so if your windows are not bullet proof, they deserve storm boards when things are starting to look ugly. If you have a wooden boat, you may prefer to keep some plywood and big nails handy and just nail the windows up if they break.

PUMPS

However good your arrangements for keeping the sea outboard, there is always a possibility of flooding, so every boat must have at least two effective pumps. One or more of these must be manually operated and one should work mechanically, either directly from the engine, or electrically.

Note that a flat-bottomed modern cruiser often has little or no bilge. In the event of taking on a quantity of water, not only will this guarantee wet bunks, but the pumps will not be able to suck unless the boat is put on an even keel, which may be inconvenient if the crew are engaged in a life or death beat off a lee shore. A boat intended for all-weather cruising should therefore have a suitable bilge. Unfortunately, this discounts many boats marketed for the purpose. We all have different priorities and flat-floored yachts have many attractive qualities. I can only pass on the warning and leave readers to decide on what's important.

HAND PUMPS

These must display the following features:

- Big capacity: 35 gallons per minute minimum, no matter how small the boat.
- Big handle: It is no good having a wonderful hand pump if it has a cartoon handle exerting no more leverage than an egg spoon. The handle must have its own stowage near the pump for obvious reasons.
- Comfortable siting: You need to be comfortable while operating a hand pump. If the electrics fail, you may end up having to work it for a long time. Many production cruisers have a dinky handle stuck discreetly in a corner. If you can't go on pumping for fifteen minutes or more at good rate, the device is a waste of time. Re-site it, and if the

handle is too short, buy a length of pipe and make up a proper one.

- Readily clearable: Nearly all pumps can clog. It is vital that the guts are easily accessible. You may need to clear it in a hurry. Try it. Have you got spare valves, diaphragms or impellers?
- Strum boxes: It can take as little as a matchstick to knock out a pump which stands alone between you and the liferaft. A good filter or strum box at the suction end will go a long way towards making sure this doesn't happen but remember that, when the boat is flooded, the water will pick up a load of extra debris from the lockers. Anything can choke a strum so be sure that every item with a high clogging capacity is well-stored.

Check the sitting of the bilge pump. Could you sit there and pump the boat dry? If not, re-site it

POWER-DRIVEN PUMPS

An engine-driven pump or an electric pump has the priceless advantage that it will work unattended, meaning that if you are looking for a leak or sorting out a shambles on deck the bilge is still being cleared. Electric pumps are reliable, cheap to buy and easy to fit, given a suitable skin fitting.

They also require no servicing beyond unclipping them from their base plates to clear the suction in the event of clogging. With a deep-bilged boat, having two or more of these at different levels, perhaps with the upper ones powered through float switches, makes perfect sense. Such pumps are tireless, but must not be relied upon exclusively.

BUCKETS

When the world goes mad and all else has failed it is amazing how much water can be moved by using the poor man's pump. The more buckets the merrier. Every sea-going yacht must have at least two, and in an ideal world there would be one for every crew member plus one or two spares. A chain can then be formed to bucket water out of the boat. Four people working efficiently may be able to move up to fifty gallons per minute this way.

Remember that if you have a self-draining cockpit the water only has to get outside the bridge deck into the self-draining cockpit to be dumped overboard so there's no need to tip it over the side.

Heavy-duty rubber buckets with metal handles from building materials' suppliers are the best value. Don't buy the huge ones. They're too heavy to handle when full. They are also unwieldy and a problem to stow.

THE RUDDER

Since the honest steering oar was abandoned a thousand or so years ago, and particularly in recent years, rudders have been causing trouble. When you consider the forces to which they are subjected it's not surprising. The shearing strain on the shaft of a big spade rudder as it passes through its bottom bearing is enormous. It's hard to excuse fitting such an arrangement into a cruising yacht, but it's not difficult to understand why designers do it. These rudders are hydro-dynamically efficient and, being easily installed without all the expense of building a hull with a full keel or skeg, they are cheap. Unfortunately, they are also very vulnerable, and many have failed. If you are stuck with one, all you can do is to ensure that the shaft and its bearings are sufficiently overbuilt and well maintained so that they can never be a source of worry.

It is safer to buy a boat with at least two beefy rudder bearings, one of which is at or near the bottom of the shaft, and then service them regularly.

A big spade rudder exerts a huge force on its pivot in a seaway

The bottom bearing of a skeg greatly strengthens the rudder

Supported throughout its length, this is the strongest of all

WHEELS

Too many wheel steering systems fail in action. No properly balanced aft-cockpit yacht under 50 feet long should need a wheel, but they are now specified for virtually every sailing boat over 30 feet. Centre cockpit boats have no choice in this matter and nor, I suspect, do boats so wide in the stern that they must have two rudders to make sure that one at least remains in the water when heeled. This is a pity for the deep-water cruiser because windvane self-steering is so much easier to rig to a tiller and in-harbour manoeuvring is more rapid and a lot more accurate, but we are where we are and must make the best of things. It's therefore incumbent on us to check all cables, fittings, blocks, quadrants and the rest of the paraphernalia, particularly when it is new, for that is when most fail. Thereafter it must be done as often as seems necessary. It's usually difficult to gain access to steering wires, and some sheave pins may be near impossible to reach, so a can of aerosol grease is a godsend for lubricating impossible places. Available from your local motor factor.

There must also be a readily accessible and properly functioning emergency tiller, which can be attached rapidly direct to the rudder stock if the wheel steering fails. I have sailed on boats where the emergency tiller thoughtfully supplied by the manufacturer literally could not be fitted for lack for space. However, on a modern yacht with a below-decks electronic autopilot, help is at hand. Most of these work by means of a ram that operates directly onto the steering quadrant, side-stepping the wheel steering system altogether. It is thus sometimes possible to steer such a boat to safety using the autopilot instead of the wheel. The arrangement may lack the pin-point accuracy of the official steering, but if you can get close enough to a dock, you can just take off all way and heave a line ashore.

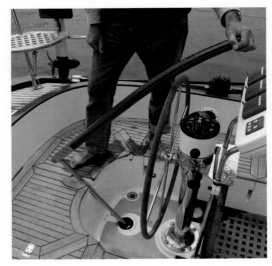

An emergency tiller

THE RIG

A yacht's rig needs to do two things. It has to be able to drive the boat through any state of wind and sea in which the hull is capable of being driven, and it mustn't fall over while doing so.

If the designer has done his job properly the rig should be able to deliver the basic requirements of propulsion. How well it works and whether or not it fails in the process is often up to the crew.

SAILS & REEFING

To be safe at sea in all weathers a boat must have a decent suit of sails in sound condition. Techniques for sail handling will be discussed in Chapter 4. Right now, we'll take a look at the options available to most of us.

HEADSAILS

Almost every yacht today has a roller-reefing headsail. This is very convenient and is a big improvement over the old hanked-on suit of sails with one for every wind strength and a lot of work to change

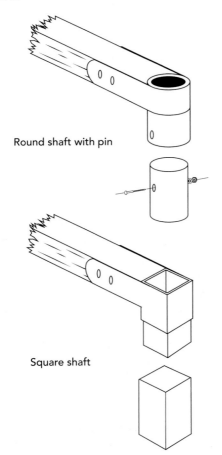

Round shaft with pin

Square shaft

If you have wheel steering, make sure the end of the rudderstock will accept an emergency tiller

the sails in between. There was also the inescapable fact that whatever sail you chose, it rarely seemed to be the right one. All that has disappeared with the roller furler.

The roller-reefed headsail has made it so much easier to reduce sail area forward of the mast

There is, of course, a trade-off. If the sail is to pull the yacht to windward in a blow, it must be specially cut for the job. Such a sail may work after a fashion when heavily reefed. If it isn't a specialist, by the time the sail is rolled into jib – let alone storm-jib – size it will set rather like a bin bag and be about as effective.

If the jib hasn't been cut for the job, it will be the wrong shape when heavily reefed

If you expect your share of heavy weather, try to avoid the temptation to order a 150% genoa. A 110% sail that's well-cut does the job almost as well in light going and, when the chips are down, it will reef a whole lot better, especially if cut with this in mind.

The best answer is to use a smaller genoa backed up by a Code Zero light-weather sail to be set when needed. Such sails are independent of the roller system and so are easy to deploy without compromising the ultimate safety of the boat.

With the genoa fully furled, a storm jib can be set

A happy compromise available to cutter owners is to set up the jib / genoa as a roller-reefer for convenience but to have the staysail set on its inboard stay as a conventional and bomb-proof headsail, possibly with a reef in it. It can then be used on its own in really heavy going, balancing nicely with deep-reefed main or trysail (or mizzen if the boat is a ketch) and setting perfectly, no matter how hard it may blow.

On my own cutter, I have my staysail on a roller as well as the genoa. When the wind pipes up above force 6, I roll away the genoa and kiss my troubles goodbye with a perfectly setting staysail ready to go at the pull of a rope. I can roller reef it a long way without spoiling its shape if I ever really need to, which is rare indeed.

Prepared for heavy weather

THE MAINSAIL

This must be capable of being reefed down quickly to about half its luff length while still maintaining a good shape. In-boom reefing is a fine solution so long as it is quality gear. Some are better than others and anything with a fixed vang is to be discounted on sight.

In-boom reefing

In-mast reefing is not ideal but, like the roller genoa, it scores highly in convenience. However, by definition, since the camber of the sail (the curvature which produces the aerofoil and the drive) is a short way forward of halfway from luff to leech, it follows that when the sail is heavily reefed, the drive will have been largely reefed out of it.

In-mast reefing

The third option, which was really the default in the twentieth century, is slab reefing with the tack and clew pulled down to the boom independently. When properly set up, this guarantees a good sail shape and is very reliable. However, unless specifically organised to avoid this, it does involve leaving the cockpit – not what most people want when the going gets tough.

Slab reefing

An innovation developed to make slab reefing operable from the safety of the cockpit is so-called single-line reefing. Unfortunately, it does little to help in really bad weather because it often results in only two reefs being available. This is not enough in a modern yacht. If a third reef can be scrambled in, it will certainly involve leaving the cockpit which is what the system is meant to avoid. Standard single-line reefing has further downsides and is not recommended for serous sailing.

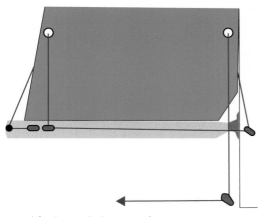

Simplified single-line reefing: Many variants include blocks inside the boom increasing friction

THE TRYSAIL

A very important part of any yacht's sail wardrobe, especially if she has issues putting in a really deep reef. In the case of some boats whose helm becomes dangerously unbalanced at the great angles of heel produced by sudden gusts, it is vital. I know of one popular 32-foot performance cruiser with a flattish bottom and 'fin and spade' configuration that sails along happily in a force 7/8 with a trysail but whose manners deteriorate dreadfully under deep-reefed main.

Trysails – classic yachts (bottom) with huge mainsails sometimes use a trysail for passage making between races

Trysails are good news because they don't use the boom, so if this should be disabled, all is not lost. They can be smaller than the deep-reefed main, providing another 'gear' to change down into, and they are always 'fresh out of the bag'. They don't get much use, so they shouldn't blow out, although this benefit carries the downside that we all forget the details of rigging that are rarely used. In other words, we need to take them out every so often to remember how they work and make sure any extra gear is to hand.

One final point: like a storm jib, there is no reason why a trysail should not be made from fluorescent orange cloth. This is another bonus from the trysail bag because white gets lost in the wave-tops in a gale and you might just as well increase your chances of being noticed.

If you aren't going across an ocean and the extra gear for a trysail you may never use seems too much trouble or expense, a really deep reef in a slab main will provide a useful substitute, but the sail must be in prime condition so there are no concerns about it blowing out, and the reef must be deep. A good in-boom main just goes on

rolling down, delivering a perfect shape all the way.

STANDING RIGGING

If your sails and gear are in order you have only to ensure that the rig stays in the boat. Spars, blocks, wire, rigging screws (turnbuckles), clevis pins, cotter pins, tee-terminals and all the rest are the easiest things on a boat to check, because you can see them. This is just as well, for failure of one is liable to lead to the loss of all and maybe the ship into the bargain.

Failure of 1x19 standing rigging

At sea, check around the gear you can reach from the deck systematically each day. Whenever possible send a volunteer aloft to do the same in harbour. When this isn't convenient because the boat is bounding from wave-top to wave-top, it is a good plan to check aloft each morning and evening with the ship's binoculars. It's surprising how much this can reveal, and you may spot a stranding wire just in time to save the day. You can find out more about using binoculars in my YouTube video.

Really deep slab reef in a mainsail

(Scan to watch this video) ↗

It must be said that if standing rigging is going to fail in use, the most likely time is when the boat falls off a wave and wrenches herself in heavier weather than she normally encounters. Stainless steel wire is prone to unpredictable failure. Its service life is rarely specified for the simple reason that a boat sailing round the world in high latitudes is going to induce a whole lot more metal fatigue than one sailing on summer days in flat water.

The best rule of thumb for boats seeing average leisure use is to replace stainless steel rigging every ten years. Insurers seem to like this being done. It may not be strictly necessary for all boats, but predicting failure by inspection is so hit-and-miss that you may feel prudence is the best policy.

THE ENGINE

For any cruising boat except for the very few who still choose to do without, the engine is an important part of her ability to handle heavy weather.

Now that petrol (gasoline) has been discounted on sensible safety grounds, there are three types of engine available to today's cruising yacht: inboard diesel, electric and outboard.

Unless they are installed in a purpose-built well, situated within the boat's load waterline, **outboard engines** can be discounted as being of any use to a yacht at sea. They are handy for scuttling around in flat water, but given even a moderate chop, the propeller comes out of the water and the average outboard arrangement becomes worse than useless.

The only thing that needs to be said about outboards in connection with heavy weather – whether prime propulsion units or just for the dinghy – is that the fuel tank must be firmly sealed, including its air vent screw. If you take a knockdown (an event

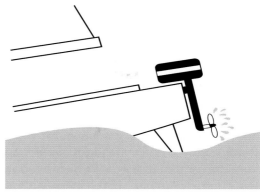

Outboard engines are of little use when the sea gets rough, and merely distract the helmsman from the business of steering the boat

more likely to occur in the smaller type of boat in which outboards tend to be fitted) you don't need fuel wandering around the boat to add to your problems.

An **inboard diesel engine** must start readily at all times, and it must keep running. There are no marine engines available nowadays which are fundamentally unreliable. Given a reasonable installation, if they become so, it is on account of slap-happy maintenance or no maintenance at all.

STARTING

If, like most units today, an engine cannot be hand started it is vital that it is equipped with a completely isolated engine battery. Without battery power there is no engine, so this must be available in profusion 24/7. All terminals should be kept tight and spotlessly clean.

Any solenoid pump cut-offs (the device that stops a diesel with the starter key instead of a separate 'pull' stop cable) should be regularly inspected. If this fails in the 'stop' mode, which can and does happen, you will probably flatten your batteries before you have sorted out what on earth is the matter.

DIRTY FUEL

Heavy weather will always search out any engine-stopping dirt that has accumulated in the fuel system.

I once crossed the English Channel in a fine old vessel that had operated for years in the Solent with never a hiccup from her engine. Thirty miles out it died, strangled by the filth of ages stirred up from the bottom of the tanks by the rough sea. There were no spare filters, so we had no engine. Fortunately we did have plenty of sea room and a reasonable sailing performance so no harm was done, but different circumstances might have given us cause to regret the lack of maintenance that led to this.

The diesel bug forming between the fuel and water

PROPELLERS

In a tumbling, turbulent sea there is no doubt that a slow-turning three-bladed propeller is far more useful than a two-bladed egg whisk, particularly one which folds. It is all very well having a 35hp engine but that power must be transmitted to the water. A small propeller cavitating frantically just below and sometimes above the surface isn't going to succeed on a rough night.

Fortunately, there is now a good choice of feathering or otherwise 'disappearing' 3-bladed units on the market. These include the 'Max-prop' and the innovative and highly effective 'Brunton Autoprop'.

Brunton's self-pitching 'Autoprop' has proper blade twist and adjusts its pitch to the thrust being transmitted

ELECTRIC POWER

The world is slowly turning towards electric power. For a short-range yacht it is an attractive option for obvious reasons. While various increasingly efficient systems for onboard charging are coming on stream at the time of writing, many years will pass before the great bogey-man of electric power, the range, will be overcome. Therefore, if you have an electric motor, you must be ready to take on heavy weather without auxiliary power, because the unit may not keep running for as long as you'd like it to. There's nothing inherently wrong with this. It's just an attitude of mind, although for a modern yacht of limited dynamic stability, it may remove one deep-water survival option from her portfolio.

THE REST

Once you are confident that hull, rig, and engine are truly seaworthy, all that remains is to ensure that everything moveable in the ship is in good order and is either permanently secured or capable of being properly stowed should the need arise. I was once advised by an old salt that as long as I prepared my boat for sea on the basis that she would at some time be flung on her beam ends, or further, I would not go far wrong.

That advice will always be sound and a vessel setting forth should hope for the best but prepare for the worst.

SECURING DOWN BELOW

Most governing bodies of the sailing world now issue codes of practice for small commercial vessels and yachts that make sure they are well-found in this respect. Although you may not legally be obliged to do so if you aren't plying for hire, you could fare no better than to take such standards to heart. In truth, however, all you really need to do is to go carefully through your boat and look at every item through the eyes of that supreme pessimist (or was he perhaps a realist?), my old salt.

You'll find all heavy items of particular interest. A 100 amp-hour 12-volt battery, for example, landing on the inhabitant of the quarter berth, could extend his watch below into eternity. Low-flying ballast pigs make neat holes in the furniture, and good solid floorboards in free fall make a dreadful racket when they hit the deckhead, so all but the smallest inspection hatches should be fastened. Unsecured locker lids turn a well-planned dinner into a premature lottery and should the cooking stove take the opportunity to jump its gimbals it will probably spray the happy home with flammable LPG gas as it enjoys a thoroughly smashing time.

No need to go on, is there?

SECURING ON DECK

Working from the basis that all deck hamper, such as boathooks, brooms, dinghies and the rest, are normally well lashed down, there are one or two extra items requiring attention before the boat starts to jump about.

Water ingress is now of prime concern. Secure the forehatch (easily forgotten), and also any other openings which may have been left 'cracked' for ventilation. Seal all air vents except proper 'dorade' boxes and check cockpit lockers. The anchor chain pipe is a source of water entry in many boats, so bung it up with a rag and a plastic bag if you've nothing better.

Any spare anchors should be below by this time and if you have one that is permanently stowed over the bow roller make sure it is solidly lashed or pinned, in the interests of both safety and quietness. No boat enjoys all that weight right out at the bow, but if you anchor frequently and sail always in sheltered waters, it makes sense to leave it thus stowed. Otherwise, it should come inboard. Whatever decision is taken, nobody wants it clattering about on its roller.

Flags don't last long if left flying in a gale so, for the sake of economy, lower them in good time. You'll also save some precious windage.

Leaving flags up in a gale is unnecessary windage and they won't last long

Spray dodgers are a source of great comfort in moderately windy weather but once the waves start breaking, they should be stowed down below. I once took a heavy sea in a dodger lashed between two through-bolted lifeline stanchions. The stanchions carried away and so strong was the dodger that they took a couple of deck planks with them. Never again!

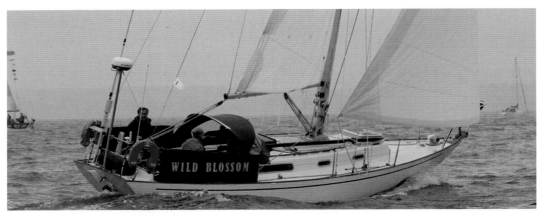

Spray dodgers are a liability when the breeze is really up

Wherever your storm sails are stowed they must be easily accessible and folded neatly, predictably and in such a manner that bending them on in a gale is at least possible. It's also a good idea to pack any blocks or sheets in the sail bag. When trysail time comes along, morale can easily be cracked by opening up and finding a big 'bunch of b*****s' instead of a willing ally.

DEALING WITH BREAKAGES

The strains imposed by heavy weather tend to multiply the chances of gear failure, and unlike the motorist, the sailor who 'breaks down' on passage cannot grab the mobile and dial-up assistance. The essence of seafaring is self-reliance and every boat which presumes to put to sea should be able to solve her own problems from within her own resources.

TOOLS

There is only one standard to apply to a toolkit for a boat venturing offshore: she must carry whatever tools are necessary to affect a temporary repair on any part of her hull, machinery or equipment.

SPARES

Any vital item which cannot be fabricated on board, and which is liable to fail, should be backed up by a suitable spare. Unfortunately, lack of stowage space and finance often compromise this ideal, but there are many small items which can be carried conveniently which could well save the day.

PLUMBING & ELECTRICAL

These are areas where nobody can specify what's going to go wrong, so a well-stocked electrical box and a plumbing bag with useful terminals, various pieces of piping, a varied supply of hose clips will usually keep things going.

BOLTS & SCREWS

Collecting a good 'fastenings box' is a lifetime's work. Having the right bolt 'in stock' should be a matter of pride for all skippers.

ROPE & 'STRING'

A boat cannot carry too much cordage. Lots of small stuff in the 'string bag' will give you a choice of materials when you need to produce a lash-up. A few coils of Dyneema for long-term lashings and the same stuff on a larger gauge for repairing standing rigging in lieu of wire.

Wire remains useful in spite of the rise of low-stretch, light-weight super-strong cordage. Galvanised fencing wire is cheap and can be obtained in suitable quantities from your local farmers' co-operative. This can also be used, stranded if necessary, as seizing wire to mouse shackles.

A plentiful supply of duct or 'gorilla' tape is also a winner in a tight corner. It sticks to almost anything and is immensely strong once a few turns are on. Make sure you have some on board, you never know when it will come in handy.

'JUNK'

In addition to official spares a boat needs all sorts of items for which, just at the moment, you can find no use. If you suffer a failure of major proportions, the most obscure piece of junk may be the one thing which, suitably modified, will get you going again.

How many lengths of timber, bent shackles, old inner tube, pieces of aluminium and mysterious rusty artefacts you carry is largely a matter of character. Some of us are squirrels at heart, others abhor the inevitable mess somewhere in the boat, but whether you love rubbish or hate it, one day you'll need it. Oh, and don't forget a couple of spare LED flashlights…

There is nothing about preparing a yacht for sea that a conscientious and observant person cannot achieve by the application of common sense. There are no mysteries and few clever tricks, just a realistic appraisal of how different everything is when the dock is far behind, the wind is piping up and you are on your own in the wild dark night. That is when you meet yourself and your work face to face and thank the Lord you replaced that dodgy shackle.

AN ALL-WEATHER TOOLKIT

The tools a boat will need before her skipper can say that she is equipped to deal with any emergency will depend upon her type, her size, the material of her hull, and many other variables. However, in addition to the obvious ones, there are a few extra items that many experienced sailors have found to be indispensable in an emergency. These are mostly the sort which will exert large amounts of power where space and time may be at a premium. Here are some examples:

☐ An extra-large adjustable wrench
☐ A medium-sized pipe wrench (Stillson)
☐ A length of hollow steel pipe to slip over the end of heavier tools in order to achieve an irresistible leverage
☐ A one-handed sledge, or lump, hammer
☐ A hefty cold chisel, kept good and sharp
☐ A number of hardwood wedges
☐ A steel wedge
☐ A dozen or so 6in, 8in, and 10in nails
☐ A small two-handed axe

☐ A set of bolt-croppers
☐ A wrecking bar

For a more definitive run-through of a sensible tool kit for a medium-range yacht, visit my YouTube Channel.

Scan to watch this video

3
THE CREW

'Ships are all right, it's the men in them...'

That remark was made in the long night before female suffrage. For our purposes, despite what my wife says, I think we can safely extend it to include both sexes and restate that no matter how well prepared our boats may be, they are only as good as their crews.

Crews vary enormously as to their resilience and ability. Often it is only when the going gets tough that we discover who we have taken aboard, even sometimes if they are members of the family, but whatever their strengths and weaknesses, all will respond to thoughtful treatment.

FOOD

There is nothing so important to a crew battling through a gale than regular, satisfying meals. Not only do they fortify the soul and fuel the body, they are also a natural mark of the passage of time, a social event, and about the only thing apart from your bunk that you've got to look forward to. It is a sign that morale is on the slide when the skipper says 'Don't bother about getting supper – it's every man for himself in the galley now.'

Routine is of tremendous importance and a good cook is a jewel beyond price. If there is no official cook and the rota is in danger of collapsing from intermittent seasickness, then it is time to call for volunteers. Volunteers, mark you, not martyrs. Perhaps because they were so critical for morale, sailing-ship cooks were referred to as 'doctor'. The skipper will need to adjudicate and may well end up as 'doctor' himself for a while.

Cooking in rough weather is an art, but a few simple devices and techniques can keep the cook safe and generally assist in the battle against what can appear hopeless odds.

■ Cooks must be protected from the stove by a solid bar between them and their charge. If the galley is set athwartships, they also need a 'bum strap' into which they can nestle coyly when the yacht lurches and they are rolled away from the task in hand.

- Wear bib-type oilskin bottoms. I know one lady personally whose legs still bear testimony to an unexpected knockdown.

Wear bib-type oilskin bottoms when cooking in heavy weather

- Use deep cooking vessels – don't mess around with that assassin, the frying pan. All pans must be clamped to the stove with their handles turned inwards. Don't rely on the gimbals alone. They won't help you if sixteen-stone Sammy, the demon winch grinder, is hurled down the ladder and into the soup.
- In extremis, use only a pressure-cooker unpressurised but with the lid clamped on. If this leaps into the cook's lap, he may be able to field it before it scalds him to death.
- Whistling kettles with no lid are a good, safe option.
- Keep meals simple and, if possible, easily

washed up. Carry special hard weather rations, but if all else fails, there is always the `five-day stew'. Leave what's not eaten in the pan and toss in something else tomorrow. Every addition brings fresh delights to the cockpit gourmets. Give it a new name each meal, perhaps to coincide with developing events. 'Casserole de la grande pooping', 'Soupe des plongeurs' or even the ultimate, 'Bare pole bisque'.

Five-day stew re-emerging for day 2

- Serve hot drinks in big mugs, half-full. Not only do full mugs spill, but the contents blow off the top and into your face.

A warm drink is a godsend on a rough night

If possible, soup and a roll is even better!

- Have a 'greedies' box full for the night watches (chocolate bars, pieces of cake, crocodile sandwiches – whatever they fancy).
- Help the victims to keep their meals down by giving preference to readily digested foods. Avoid rice salads with raw peppers and suchlike delicacies. They are just as colourful on their second viewing and their return will sap the morale of all.
- And finally, the best tip of all. Before going below or rising from the safety of the bunk to cook, plan meticulously everything you need to do. Recall where everything is and have a list of actions in your mind. When that's all in place, take a deep breath and go for it. Hanging onto a strap in the galley trying to think what to do next is a sure-fire passport to the sickbay.

SEASICKNESS

This is often the biggest problem facing any crew in bad weather. Very few people are completely immune, even if the more fortunate only feel queasy and lazy. Heavy sufferers soon become convinced that only death can provide relief. These are likely to remain of no use to the ship until either the passage of time or arrival in port ends their misery.

With suitable encouragement some chronic sufferers are able to stand their watches and even enjoy themselves between bouts. Others throw in the towel and give up. For anyone, careful pacing helps tremendously.

If you are feeling sick, remember that the best position to adopt is flat out in your bunk, with a bucket alongside if necessary. You will feel much better. Resist the temptation to stay on deck whatever the odds because that is the road to exposure and complete moral breakdown.

Flat out on the bunk

It may go against the grain of good housekeeping, but don't even think about trying to get undressed for the bunk. Never mind making yourself ill struggling into the stripey pyjamas. Just 'turn in all standing' with your oilskins on. Pull a duvet or a sleeping bag over you and get your head straight down. Struggling out of bib-front bottoms gives the seasick fairy every chance of creeping up on you. Don't worry about getting the cushions damp. They will dry in due course and it's more important right now to look after yourself. You may feel worse initially down below, but as soon as you are prone, things will improve. You may even drop into a doze which passes the time wonderfully. Then when you are needed, you will be ready and as fit as you are likely to be.

Try to eat if you can face it, otherwise don't. 'Sick bics' (dry, arrowroot biscuits) and water are a good start. Ginger seems to work well, either in biscuit form or crystallised.

If you are a seasick skipper, you'll need to keep your navigating efforts to an efficient minimum because nothing churns the stomach like peering at a wet chart that's bouncing around (see Chapter 5) or struggling with the intricacies of a plotter menu.

Watch your crew carefully for signs of seasickness: yawning, pallor, lack of interest and refusal to go below are all pointers to the approaching first vomit. Try giving a prospective sufferer an easy job, particularly steering. Often, they'll pull back from the brink, but even if this doesn't save the day, don't let them fall overboard as they throw up. People being seasick lose all interest in everything else, including personal survival.

If someone is suffering from seasickness, give them an easy job, like steering

SEASICKNESS REMEDIES

One hundred and fifty years before the first serious efforts were made to handle seasickness with medication, Charles Darwin wrote to his father, '... if it was not for seasickness, the whole world would be sailors.' This remark held good until immediately after World War II, when a chance discovery led to the development of the antihistamine drug, Dramamine, as a cure for motion sickness. This, and other similar drugs, are generally taken orally and, for many people, undoubtedly ease the situation. Their main drawback is that they attack the symptom, which emanates from the balance control centre at the base of the brain, rather than the cause, which is disorientation of the body's main balance sensory mechanism in the inner ear. In the doses required to prevent or cure seasickness these drugs tend to produce undesirable side-effects, such as drowsiness and a feeling of dryness in the mouth.

Late in the 1970s a new and more effective medication, Cinnarizine became available. This worked directly on the cause of the problem in the inner ear. Like the antihistamines this is also taken in tablet form and has been on the market for some time as 'Stugeron'. Its arrival has made such a difference to the offshore yachting scene that one wishes it could have been offered to the unhappy Mr Darwin, who wrote his letter home from the pit of despair after a week in the Bay of Biscay. I have run a long-term experiment with many different crews using seasickness medications of the 'Stugeron' type and they proved to be effective for most people when used as directed. Don't reach for the medicine when you are already feeling ill. Read the instructions a couple of days before you put to sea, start taking the pills early and do not listen to the bombast of certain individuals for whom they have not worked – very likely because they did not follow orders.

A more recently available source of relief comes in the form of slow-release 'patches' which adhere to the skin. Most of these carry either Dramamine or Scopolamine, both of which commonly induce tiredness. If you don't want chemical drugs, herbal patches can be sourced on the internet, but I have no idea how well they work.

Two things should be borne in mind here. The first, as with all medicines, is to read the leaflet in the box about side-effects. Apart from the usual caveats regarding pregnancy, etc., the most common is likely to be drowsiness. I've met people who say, 'I'm not taking that. It makes you sleepy.' Clearly these innocents have never been seasick. If they had, they would understand my answer. 'Which would you rather be? Drowsy, or wish you were dead ...'

Stugeron: effective for most people when used as directed

PERSONAL INJURY

Once a small boat begins to jump about, she becomes an unusually dangerous environment. The possibilities for injury are many so one or more of her crew should be qualified to treat damaged personnel by having at least attended a basic first-aid course.

Most of the injuries sustained in yacht accidents are predictable and preventable. The skipper should be looking out all the time to make sure the crew do not make those mistakes which are likely to result in their being hurt. Here are some of the favourites:

- Burns and scalds in the galley: totally unnecessary if the precautions on page 41 are heeded.
- A sharp bang on the head from a flogging headsail clew or sheet. Don't let a sail flog with anyone near it; if it is unavoidable, warn the prospective victim to keep his or her head out of the way.
- In recent years the question of being hit on the head by the boom has had its full share of publicity and it is true that booms have been the cause of a number of cranial injuries, some of them fatal. The campaign for 'hard hats for yachtsmen' seems to have faded out, as well it should if we are to retain any freedom at all. Nonetheless, the skipper must be aware of this head-bashing piece of gear, particularly in hard conditions when tacking, or where there is the slightest danger of an involuntary gybe. If in doubt, warn your crew.
- Mainsheet tracks in the cockpit are falling out of fashion in cruising boats, but there are always going to be plenty around for the simple reason that they make setting the sail more efficient. Keep folks well away from these hazards

when sailing off the wind, especially in a big sea where a broach is possible. If you gybe without making fast both sides of the traveller, or if the jammer on the car tackle should fail, the car will whip across the track mincing everything in its path. If the car misses, the sheet itself is most effective at smashing spectacles on the face, breaking expensive dentures or throwing the unsuspecting around like rag dolls, inflicting far more serious head injuries. Secure both sides of the traveller at all times. And watch the boom!

Secure both sides of the traveller at all times

- Rope burns. These are usually caused by inexperienced crew removing a round turn from a cleat or a winch, so the sufferer is left holding a live, loaded rope. Don't let anyone commit such an atrocity.
- Crushed fingers or worse caused by playing fast and loose with ground tackle and particularly chain cable. Be on the watch for inexperienced hands unaware of the deadly danger. It's not difficult to lose a foot from being casual in this respect, and there are four-fingered sailormen everywhere.

Ground tackle is always ready to grab a foot or a finger

- Broken or dislocated fingers where a rope has picked up on an engagement or signet ring. Rings should be removed at sea as they have caused a number of such accidents.
- Broken bones caused by being thrown around, particularly down below. Fit plenty of solid grab handles where they are most needed.
- Falling down the companionway. Remind everyone to take their time. A broken pelvis from this accident is the nightmare of every single or two-hander.

The companionway is another injury trap – everyone should take their time

- If you enjoy sailing barefoot you need to accept the odd broken toe with a straight face. Modern boats are veritable minefields of projections for the careless naturist.
- Never let the ship's engineer lean into the engine compartment wearing any loose clothing. An open shirt cuff may be caught by a whirling fan belt, or a sportily hanging scarf could take a turn around the drive for the injector pump. The first may do no more than rip the garment from his back, but the effects of the second are depressing in the extreme.
- The injuries resulting from attempts to fend off one vessel from another (even a dinghy) or a vessel from a wall can be awful. The skipper must not allow anyone to try this. Even a three-ton yacht builds up far more momentum than a strong man can absorb in the space available. If the fenders are not to hand, you'll have to grit your teeth and bear the crunch. Better to damage your capping rail than lose a limb.

If the fenders aren't to hand, don't try to fend off a vessel with momentum

- The dinghy. By far the greatest number of drownings among cruising yachtsmen occur between ship and shore. The dinghy is a dangerous place, particularly in a heavy blow. Now is the time to make sure all hands wear their lifejackets. It seems to me that a slavish rote of lifejacket-wearing for good swimmers in stable dinghies in perfect conditions can lead only to contempt for a too-rigid rule. Save your authority until it matters, and then insist. The other occasion to insist, even on a calm night, is when the crew come back from the pub. This has nothing necessarily to do with heavy weather, but it should be noted that the booze has claimed even more victims than the gale when it comes to dinghy work.

Insist on lifejackets when coming back from the pub, even on a calm night

SAFETY HARNESSES & LIFEJACKETS

Every crew member should have a lifejacket and tether

Without a doubt the most valuable pieces of safety gear on the ship are the safety harnesses. Every crew member should be issued with a tether and a lifejacket at the outset of a passage and each should adjust it to fit correctly, with the 'pulling point' on the apex of the breastbone and the crotch strap secure.

All skippers will make their own rules about when lifejackets should be used, and when harnesses are to be deployed. Some authorities insist on lifejackets on deck at all times. I've even heard requirements to wear one on stepping from the shore onto a marina pontoon. If this appeals, then go with it. However, such draconian 'universal' rules do not strike me as realistic. Try telling anybody who habitually sails in warm waters that he or she must wear an approved lifejacket at all times and see what response you get!

Given average ability to swim, to don a lifejacket and take it off every time one goes below in fair weather seems to me to be absurd, never mind the obvious drawbacks of wearing a lifejacket complete with crotch strap over a bathing suit. The best of modern lifejackets are very unobtrusive, however, and there's no doubt that if the unthinkable were to happen and you were to take a dive, wearing one properly would give you a better chance, so it comes down to personal choice for much of the time. In heavy weather, all this changes.

If all hell is breaking loose, then clipping on to a carefully sited strong point in the cockpit before leaving the companionway and staying clipped on until you are back down below again makes complete sense. The clipping on is vital because the important thing isn't to float if you do fall over, but not to fall overboard in the first place. Since today's harnesses are one

In heavy weather, clip on before leaving the companionway

with the neat, stowable lifejacket, you may as well wear that as well. Certainly, anyone leaving the cockpit for any reason – particularly to be sick – should be attached.

In this sort of weather, I have no hesitation clipping on

In heavy weather, gents who like to obey the call of nature by direct delivery to the sea rather than via the head should be recommended to go below to attend to matters and to sit on the bowl as they do. The reasons should be obvious. If they are unwilling, insist they clip on or, if things are desperate (the weather, I mean), the cockpit drain makes an invaluable aid for the incontinent. Any splashback will be washed away by the next wave.

Boats should be equipped with jackstays running along the deck so that the crew can remain clipped to the ship all the way from the cockpit to pulpit. These are usually nylon webbing which is immensely strong and has the advantage over wire of being comparatively silent as a clip runs along it. Furthermore, unlike wire, webbing doesn't roll beneath the boot and defeat its own object by throwing you over the guardrails.

Losing a man overboard is the worst thing that can happen short of actual shipwreck. Apart from common sense and the survival instinct, the harness backed up by a lifejacket is the best assistance the skipper has for keeping the hands the right side of the wall or recovering them alive if the harness fails. No money should be spared on this gear, and there should be no relaxing of the ship's stated rules for wearing it.

WATCH SYSTEMS

It's as well to remember when deciding on a watch system that the ship comes first. The crew are there to serve the ship and if the ship arrives in safety at her destination, then those of her crew who have not died of the plague, or fallen overboard, will do so too.

The crew can only serve their ship if they are alert and strong. In bad weather, sitting for four hours at a spray-swept helm

fighting to keep the boat from broaching does not militate in favour of alertness and, after all that exertion, strength will be low on the list of the watchman's good points as well. He or she needs sleep, leisure to eat meals and plenty of time below decks to ward off the incipient exposure or even hypothermia that lurk in the cockpit.

Each crew will work out a system to suit itself, but the guiding principle should be 'a short sharp watch on deck, followed by a well-spent watch below.' This gives the ship her best chance of being efficiently served.

Making sure time below is spent well in heavy weather is a service to the ship, the rest of the crew and to yourself

SHORT-HANDED WATCH SYSTEMS

My wife and I sail two-up these days. Over the years we have found that the following system works effectively (see overleaf).

This system has served us well. Three hours is do-able on your own, given that you will have the self-steering working so you can occupy yourself with whatever you find helps you while always maintaining a proper lookout every few minutes.

1800	Happy hour followed by dinner for all
1900-2200	Evening watch
2200-0100	Middle watch
0100-0400	Graveyard watch
0400-0700	Morning watch
0700	Breakfast, followed by no formal watches until 1900. Sleep, rest, and recreation are taken according to need and conscience.

In bad weather, three hours is too much. Two hours are enough for anyone and, in extremis, we have cut the time on deck to one hour. Watches below are inevitably curtailed as well, but the blow won't go on for ever. You will be far more use to the ship after a rest – however short.

With a crew of three, the system stays the same except that instead of working watch-on-watch, we work '3 hours on, six off'. Bliss. The day situation remains the same.

With four watch keepers or more, the watch no longer needs to be stood alone, so the old sailing ships' 'four-on, four-off and dog-watches at 1600-1800 and 1800-2000' has worked well for us. The second dog is happy hour when all hands can gather for a sundowner, a yarn or an indignation meeting. With a watch of two, one can stay alert while the other takes a doze, ready on call if needed. Each watch can work this out for itself, and so the night passes and the crew stay fresh. In extreme weather, again, the watch period is shortened.

SLEEP

To give an anxious, part-time sailor unaccustomed to a bouncing, swishing 30-degree angle of heel any chance of sleep at all, a boat must be fitted with enough decent sea berths for the watch below. Solid leeboards are best because they give the greatest feeling of security, but a high lee cloth is a good second.

As you look at the gleaming vessels on sale in any boat show, you will observe that such things are becoming optional extras in many production yachts. Maybe this is an indication from the manufacturers that they do not expect their products to go to sea. If choosing a boat for offshore sailing, reject any without decent sea berths.

A saloon settee is fine, so long as it has a leeboard or cloth and a reading light. Nobody will want to sit on it at 0300, but it will be no use as a berth if it's curved. Such arrangements may work in harbour for some people, but they are a complete nuisance at sea. The same goes for armchairs. In fact, the motion of the boat is often at a minimum either low down amidships or aft. Trying to sleep forward of the mast in any but the largest yacht is no fun at all.

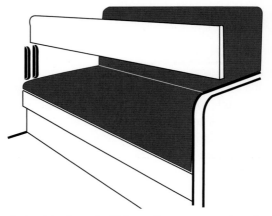

A stout leeboard will keep the weary mariner in his bunk during his watch below

CLOTHING

The advertisements and reports in the yachting press make it crystal clear that it is possible to kit yourself out with sailing gear which you will need a mortgage to pay for. It is obviously of paramount importance to keep warm and dry at sea, but it pays to remember that until sportswear became big business, people were climbing Everest in canvas anoraks and crossing the Atlantic wearing simple oilskins, souwesters and farming boots. So don't get carried away.

If you can afford the gear, buy it. It's great stuff. But don't spend money on multicoloured 'team' oilies for all the crew when you are scratching around wondering whether or not to fork out the money for a trysail.

If you wear any but the finest yachting boots, you'll have cold feet anyway. Speaking of which, modern high-end yachting boots really are worth the money. Buy a pair that's big enough to take proper socks inside.

The essential kit for heavy weather

Given good footwear, or what was known in Old Lancashire as, 'a gradely understanding', a basic heavy-weather kit should include simple, sound oilskins with high bottoms for men – my wife prefers a waist-length version for obvious reasons – and some decent keep-you-warms underneath. Modern 'middle layer' suits are undoubtedly best in this respect, but if you are starting out in life and cash is short, never forget marvellous real wool. It is available from thrift shops (the alternative chandlers), or any decent car boot sale. It is warm, it smells great and goes on doing so regardless of three-day bodies inside it. It is also worn by millions of satisfied sheep, goats and alpacas in five continents. They can't all be wrong.

Also on the subject of natural fibre in bad weather, and not to put too fine a point on it, I have found that the 'inner layer' products of most of the major marine manufacturers smell vile after wearing them for a day. B.O. isn't in it! At sea in hard going, this is totally unacceptable. By all means wear this stuff, but keep a cotton vest between it and yourself. It will last for days on end and you'll still be good for taking tea with the King when you arrive.

THE SKIPPER

It is natural to be anxious when offshore in a small boat with the weather deteriorating seriously. The crew will feel that way and so will the skipper. The way he or she behaves can have a considerable effect on the emotional state of the rest of the crowd and hence upon the efficiency with which they serve the ship.

Skippers will approach this challenge from different angles depending on their own strengths and weaknesses, but some general suggestions may be helpful for those who, like most of us, are not natural leaders:

- Take all hands into your confidence. The crew need to feel they are a team and are acting together. If you share your decision-making process with them, explaining why you are adopting your chosen course, they will feel a great deal happier. If there are those on board whose nautical judgment you value, why not discuss the reasons for your decisions? What you must not do is appear indecisive, for this is an admission that you are experiencing the anxiety which everyone else is trying to suppress. By all means share your doubts, if it helps you to resolve them quickly, but do not try to mitigate your anxieties by loading them onto others who are looking to you for strength.
- Delegate as much of the work as possible while doing your share, and then show faith in those to whom you have delegated. This will not only give you the chance to save yourself until you may be needed, it will involve more crew members in the responsible running of the ship, which assists the vital feeling of teamwork.
- Encourage weaker crew members to 'do their bit' of the watch keeping. Even someone almost too sick to care can be detailed off to look out to leeward from the shelter of the best spot in the cockpit. If he doesn't feel he is helping he begins to harbour a black mood of failure and despair. His morale sinks to the bottom of the sea and his gloomy presence upsets the rest of the hands. He will also be sheepish when it's over and you all stride ashore to boast to one another of your deeds. And that's a shame.

The ability of an outfit to deal with hard weather begins with a well-found vessel, but in the end it depends on the crew giving the ship the chance to do herself justice. When you are considering options, your correct assessment of their ability could be of vital importance. It doesn't do to ask too much from a weak group if you have the choice of another course of action, but if the same group is faced with no choice at all, then how they come through will depend to a great extent on the amount of thought you put into leading them. A little deliberation is worth a lot of brute strength.

The skipper needs to maintain morale

4

HANDLING THE BOAT

Each point of sailing brings its own challenge, but in heavy weather it is the ability to work to windward and keep going without breaking up that is the final arbiter between one boat and another. Sail shape is of vital importance to this ability.

SAILS

HEADSAILS

ROLLER GENOAS

At low wind speeds the greater the curvature, or 'belly', of a sail, the greater it's power. If you sheet your jib in too tight on a gentle day the boat dies under you. Ease the sheet, and she points just as well and comes back to life. By doing this you have put the right shape into the sail to enable it to do its job. Its maximum camber (the 'high point' of its curve) will be about 40 percent of the way from luff to leech.

Halyard tension often has a direct effect upon this curvature. Use the halyard winch to set up the camber of your sail until it is right for that wind speed; then adjust the sheet.

As the wind stiffens you will find that the camber moves aft, and the sail becomes baggy. When this happens, the sail is 'dragging' more and 'lifting' less. It is making the boat heel excessively, and it is slowing her down. To get the sail back to scratch, crank up the halyard, watching the sail carefully until the camber is back where you want it. If your sail is on a roller, once it is reefed, there will be little more to be done in this respect, so if it looks like being a windy day, put on some extra halyard tension before you start reefing.

Roller headsails are typically cut to perform best when fully unrolled in a true wind of force 3-4. It is unlikely that the aft portion which is left setting after you have rolled in the first third of the camber will come anywhere near producing the sort of lift you need. You may also be suffering a great deal of headstay sag, giving your headsail a curved luff at a time when it is crying out for a straight one.

In addition, as you roll the sail around

53

the headfoil, you create a lump of dead windage which the air has to climb around before it gets a bite on the sail itself.

All this is so unattractive that the cutter foretriangle with a dedicated staysail cut for sterner stuff than the genoa makes a lot of sense. By the time the genoa is losing its drive, the main will be reefed and the staysail can be unrolled or hoisted, to balance and drive the boat with the genoa rolled away.

STORM JIBS & 'BLADE' JIBS

Before 'storm-jib time' arrives, but when the genoa is obviously not happy in its half-rolled state, a 'blade jib' is a useful half-way house for boats with no permanent inner forestay that carries a staysail ready to hoist or unroll. In fact, when cruising in breezy places such as the Eastern Caribbean during the 'Christmas Winds', a blade can be used as the default headsail. It is tall, narrow, efficient and cut for strong winds.

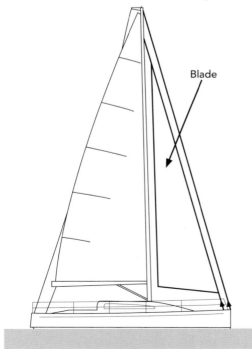

Blade

A blade jib

A storm jib is the best answer to working upwind in 30 knots plus, but, like the blade, it needs a stay to hank to because the rolled genoa is using up the main forestay. This is easy enough to arrange. The top of the stay is permanently rigged near the masthead. When not in use, the stay lives tucked away neatly in the shrouds somewhere. When its day dawns, it is secured to a strong pad-eye on the foredeck properly backed up down below. A highfield lever, a turnbuckle or, best of all, a block and tackle set it up.

A storm jib in use in the Caribbean

Both blade and storm jib must be cut so that the sheet lead works with existing gear. Given this, even the storm jib will drive a good boat to windward long after all else has failed. Like a trysail, it carries the extra benefit of always being 'fresh out of the bag'.

If rigging a storm forestay is not your cup of tea, modern materials make it possible to have a storm jib made with a strong Dyneema luff. With the sail tacked down solidly, this can be set flying and winched tight up until it is literally singing. It won't be quite as good as a stay, but with a serious halyard winch it can work perfectly well.

THE MAINSAIL

The same premises apply to mainsail shape as to headsails. At each stage of reefing, the degree and position of camber are vital.

With a modern mainsail there are plenty of controls to achieve this. Halyard, outhaul, traveller and vang (kicking strap) are minimum equipment on most cruisers nowadays.

**More outhaul + more halyard tension
= flatter sail**

The vang (kicking strap) is more interesting.

The function of the vang is to control leech tension. Ease it off and the boom rises, allowing the upper part of the leech to twist away. This twist is an important factor in how well the sail works. If there is too much twist the sail will spill wind from the upper portion, but if there is too little the upper third of the sail may stall and simply drag the boat sideways, making her heel as it does so.

A good rule of thumb for twist is to use the vang to line up the top batten of the sail with the boom when viewed from directly under the boom. This should ensure maximum lift and minimum drag. In practice the mainsheet pulls down on the leech when close-hauled and does much of the vang's work. As the boat sails further from the wind and the sail is sheeted so that it is no longer directly above the traveller, the vang comes into its own and maintains leech tension.

Once you have shaped the mainsail using halyard, outhaul, vang and sheet, you need to trim it at the correct angle to the airflow. This is where the traveller comes in. In heavy weather you will have been working to get the sail nice and flat, but if you set the traveller in the centre and ease the sheet to trim the sail, the twist will go to pieces and the sail will become fuller into the bargain. To prevent this, ease the traveller down to leeward instead of letting off the sheet. Watch the sail carefully for 'breaking' at the luff. If the boat is driving well with a good headsail and the helm feels balanced, it's not important if the sail lifts a little; however, let it lift too much and you are back to excess drag once more. Put another reef in, mate. It's about time.

SHORTENING SAIL

HEADSAILS

It is all very well to chat glibly about 'rolling in some headsail'. The mechanics of doing this are obvious enough but how to set about the job in a bad blow and not give the crew a heart attack trying to pull or winch it in is something else entirely.

First off, what about the furling line? The more yachts I sail, the more I realise how systemic unnecessarily hard pulls have become. My boat is 44ft long with a 130% masthead genoa. I am well on the long side of seventy years old, yet furling the sail in force 5 without a winch isn't a problem. If it's blowing much harder, I run off to collapse the sail in the lee of the main to help myself out. If you need a winch on anything less than 45ft, something is wrong.

Usually the difficulty lies in the furling line – too many blocks of too low a quality, especially that final one that turns the line through 120 degrees to lead it into the cockpit. What a killer! Sort out the leads so the line runs as straight as possible from drum to cockpit. Try it without that horrible last block that turns it towards a winch. You might have a nice surprise. Jammers often get in the way of a good lead too. Give it the thought it deserves because it's an important part of sailing the boat.

Now, with the lead as good as it can be, how do we make rolling it easier?

RUN OFF

The surest way to put any headsail to sleep is to blanket it behind the main. Steer as near as you dare to a dead run, easing off the mainsheet as you bear away. As soon as the genoa starts to flap around, it's lost all its power and will roll up as sweet as a lamb. It's a whole lot better than trying to fight a tiger with the sail flogging with a noise like thunder in 25 knots of wind.

REEFING THE MAINSAIL

Here again, the skipper's thoughts in bad weather should always be moving in the direction of making the job as easy as possible.

Whatever the boat or the reefing system and so long as you aren't reefing a slab sail on a dead run (see below), slowing the boat down and spilling all the wind from the mainsail always helps a lot. The best way to achieve this happy state is by 'steering shy'. Ease the mainsheet to something like a close-reaching position and then steer a touch 'above' close-hauled. The headsail will still draw sufficiently to keep way on and you can, by using the helm, slow the boat right down while maintaining control. You probably won't choose to let the speed fall much below three knots for fear of losing your grip, but it will take the sting out of the reefing job.

SLAB REEFING WITH THE WIND FORWARD

Slab reefing is a similar process in every fore-and-aft rigged boat I have ever sailed. The only notable difference against the old gaff-rigged craft where I cut my teeth is that on a modern cruiser with a five-man

crew it can be done in under 20 seconds, while on my old 30-ton gaffer it took my wife, my mate and myself about a quarter of an hour. Because it's so easy in a modern yacht such vessels can always show the breeze the right amount of sail and a husband-and-wife team should be capable of doing the job in not much more than one minute. If it takes you upwards of two then something is wrong, either with your gear or your practice.

Here's how it goes:

1. Dump the vang (kicking strap).
2. Set up the topping lift and ease away the mainsheet.
3. Ease the main halyard and either hook the new reef tack cringle to the ram's horn at the gooseneck or pull down the new tack line permanently rigged to the sail and led aft to the cockpit.
4. Set up the main halyard to tension the luff.
5. Pull down the new clew cringle using the ready-rove reef pennant (winch, tackle or manpower, the principle's the same).
6. Secure the pennant, ease away the topping lift, then set up the sheet and vang so as to flog the sail for as short a time as possible.
7. Tidy up. This may mean tying in the reef points, though on a short-boomed modern sloop this is rarely necessary except in the worst weather. Take such a liberty with a big classic mainsail, however, and I won't come to your funeral.

SLAB & SINGLE LINE REEFING WITH THE WIND FROM AFT

While it is possible to reef a headsail on any point of sailing, conventional wisdom has it that a mainsail must spill wind by shortening down, but rounding up in a near-gale to pull down a third tuck is a dramatic business best left alone. With classic slab reefing and good gear, reefing downwind can be readily achievable.

If you have to go forward to the winches, clip on and take your time. It sometimes helps to ease any boom preventer and sheet the sail in a little way to clear the spreaders, especially if these are swept aft. Set up the preventer again, keep the vang on, ease the halyard slowly and pull down the luff while a mate heaves in the clew pennant to keep the battens from blowing into the shrouds. This works surprisingly well on boats up to around 45 feet.

It's no good with single-line reefing because you can't control the leech properly and the sail will end up wrapped in the shrouds and spreaders. If this is the case, there's still no need to bring the boat head to wind. Just get everything ready, then come quickly up onto a close enough reach for the mainsail to spill wind. Now you can crank the reef down as best you can and bear away again. Not nice, but necessary.

An in-boom system manages this really quickly – see below. Not so single-line reefing which takes so long to grind all that rope down that drama sometimes results. If you've any choice in the matter, single-line reefing is not a good idea.

IN-BOOM REEFING DOWNWIND

Sadly, downwind reefing is a non-starter with many in-boom systems because it's asking too much of the universal joint at the gooseneck. The tactics here are therefore pretty standard, but preparation is the key to minimising the stress. First, set the topping lift and vang so the boom is at the critical angle it must adopt for successful reefing. On a well-found yacht, the lines will already be marked to indicate this state. Clear away the halyard and downhaul and only when fully ready, steer quickly up onto a close reach, spill wind,

ease the halyard and crank the downhaul in on the winch, maintaining luff tension with the halyard. Set the vang and topping lift smartly, then bear away. Job done in seconds. Dead easy.

In-boom reefing

REEFING IN-MAST

The technique here is identical to furling the sail. Once again, boom angle to the mast may well be critical, and keeping some tension on the outhaul while rolling in is vital in many systems. Some can be managed on any point of sailing. Others are fussier.

POINTS OF SAIL

HELMING TO WINDWARD

In rough seas any but the heaviest, most powerful boat needs sympathetic steering. The danger is that you build up speed and then literally fly off the crest of a wave to land with a nerve-shattering crash in the trough with no chance of building up speed again before the next wave stops you altogether.

Helming to windward

It is a happy coincidence that the boats most prone to this wretched habit are the ones best able to mitigate its effects. Modern, race-influenced flat-bottomed cruisers are demons for the pounding, but they are also quick and sharp on the helm, giving their drivers every opportunity to avoid the problem if they are sufficiently skilful and not tired out by the process.

The heavy displacement pre-war yacht or working vessel will be far too slow on the tiller to do much to help herself, but these boats generally have the momentum to drive on through, albeit somewhat wetly. They do not pound and they are generally easy to steer in a seaway. Hit the groove,

keep them there and they will do the rest. If the wavelength is such that a boat of this type doesn't like it, all you can do is bear away ten degrees and let her 'foot faster' to make up the lost ground. It will certainly prove a more comfortable option and may lose less time than you imagine.

The rig powers up enormously for every ten degrees further off the wind you go between 40 and 70 degrees. By the time such a vessel has settled for 55 or 60 degrees she should be unstoppable.

The technique in the lighter, quicker boats is as follows: Keep an eye on each wave as it approaches, then luff the boat gently towards the crest, bearing away sharply as you get there and sailing further off the wind down its back. Repeat the process for each wave. You will average out at a useful angle to the true wind and give your crew a tolerable ride.

The problem is that a fair degree of skill is required to do this effectively, and considerable endurance is needed to continue doing so for an extended period. It is not insignificant that top offshore racing boats carry specialist 'upwind helmsman'.

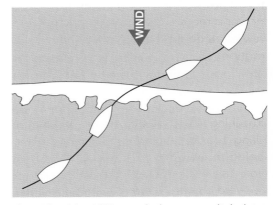

Considerable skill is needed to steer a light boat to windward in a rough sea by luffing towards the crest of each wave and bearing away down the back

Whatever you are sailing, the message is to keep her moving. High pointing will mean slow speed in heavy weather. Slow speed means excessive leeway and that is not to be tolerated.

MOTORSAILING

It is an inescapable law of physics that a close-hauled boat is developing less forward drive from a given wind than she is on any other point of sailing. In calm water this rarely presents any difficulties to a good sailing boat, but when the tremendous stopping power of a head sea is inserted into the equation, the windward performance of all but the finest yachts can deteriorate alarmingly.

When being stymied in this way, the application of a little power can make all the difference. The boat will point higher, leeway will be cut down, she will never miss her tacks and she will drive ahead in an altogether more satisfactory manner. Unless she has a really big engine, a sailing boat generally doesn't do well motoring straight into a sea but cracked off to 30 or 40 degrees with a well-reefed mainsail set, she will manage better. If pointing and heel angle is a priority, leaving the headsail rolled away will help a lot. Where absolute power is required, keep it all up, crack off a few more degrees and live with the livelier motion.

REACHING

Reaching in a steep sea is potentially dangerous on account of the possibility of being thrown down by a wave that takes you beam on. Since you are heeled to leeward anyway, it won't have far to knock you and because of this you can never carry as much sail in rough water as you would in calm, even though you need it desperately to drive you through the jumble of seas.

Reaching in heavy winds

Close-reaching, the best solution is to turn towards any evil-looking waves and then bear away down the back once more, as when sailing to windward. Any boat can do this and all types can benefit from it. It shouldn't be necessary to luff head to wind. Altering course sufficiently to take the wave on the shoulder rather than on the beam will do the trick. You'll have to duck the spray though.

On a beam reach, by far the most hazardous course, it's usually safest to bear away onto a broad reach when a nasty one comes your way.

If the wind is well abaft the beam and you are not concerned about getting to leeward of your course, an interesting option is to bear away some more, catch the wave and go surfing. This is great fun so long as you aren't anywhere near losing control and broaching. A broach can leave you beam-on to the next wave with the possibility of being knocked flat or even rolled over. Treat surfing with respect. It has its place, but you need the services of an alert, natural helmsman to be sure of your security.

RUNNING

When running at sea in hard weather the greatest danger is that of being broached by a big wave. When a boat slews round to windward the extra momentum of her turn increases her chances of a bad knockdown. If she performs the dreaded leeward broach, she has all this to contend with, plus the added bonus of an all-standing gybe. Hence the term, 'gybe-broach'.

In order to avoid these possibilities, the first action is to ensure the right amount of sail is set. Too little and you won't have proper control; too much and you will run up to your maximum hull speed and develop serious steering difficulties. Most boats steer contentedly at the sort of speed they can make to windward in calm water, which is something like the square root of their waterline sailing length in feet – about five knots for a 28-footer.

This yacht is under good control running with a deep-reefed mainsail only

If the mainsail is set, it usually makes a lot of sense to rig a strong preventer from the boom end to the bow of the boat. The ideal arrangement is to lead this through a snatch block on the foredeck and then bring it aft to a spare winch, so you can slip it from the safety of the cockpit in an emergency.

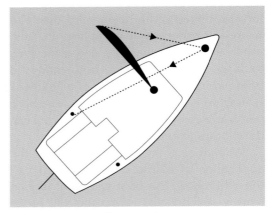

When running before a gale, rig a preventer to stop the mainsail gybing accidentally

A headsail, if the main is set, should be boomed out firmly to windward.

The important thing is that the clew should be held rigid. If it can swing about it will increase the boat's natural tendency to roll. So long as the booming-out pole is rigged with an after guy, a foreguy and a topping lift, it is perfectly triangulated and cannot move. If the sheet is led through the end of the pole and winched up short, there is no friction to chafe the rope and no tendency to roll the boat either.

When only one sail is required, some boats are quite happy to run under a deep-reefed main. Others would be difficult to steer like this and behave better with a lone headsail or 'front wheel drive' arrangement. So long as the boat is not on a dead run, the headsail may well stand without a pole, making the whole experience a great deal less physical.

STEERING THROUGH A ROLL

This an art which any dinghy helmsman will have developed, but the big-boat sailor may need advice on how best to cope. As the boat rolls to leeward she will need weather helm to hold her straight. As she comes upright and rolls up to windward, lee helm will be called for quickly to stop her careering off by the lee and gybing.

This is because the centre of effort of the rig is moving from outboard on one side of the yacht to outboard on the other, and on each side it exerts a force which, if unopposed, pulls her off course. The effect is aggravated by the natural tendency of a heeled vessel to turn towards the side on which her keel is extended.

In a dinghy, the bottom line is obvious: get it wrong and you are swimming. In most weather the cruiser will let you off lightly but in a real gale your mistake could have more drastic results.

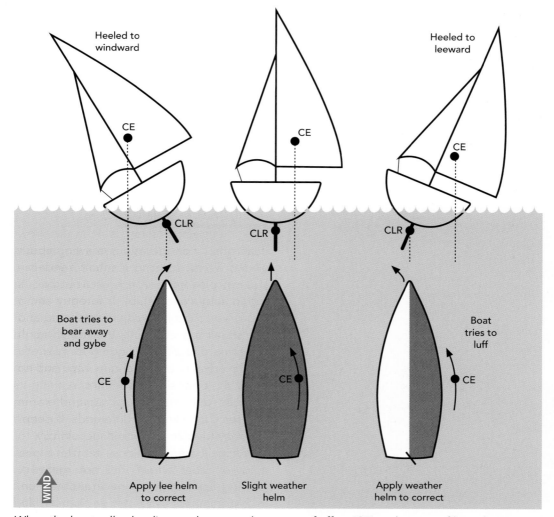

When the boat rolls, the distance between the centre of effort (CE) and centre of lateral resistance (CLR) increases, and she tries to broach

RUNNING & THE APPARENT WIND FACTOR

Running downwind, it is easy to enter a fool's paradise and completely mis-read what the wind is really doing. This is the apparent wind effect.

Put simply, a yacht running at 6 knots in 36 knots of wind subtracts her own speed from the speed of the wind. Thus, she experiences 30 knots across her deck. This is force 7, a wind one cannot ignore, but not necessarily one to write home about.

If she now turns for some reason and is obliged to sail to windward, she adds her own speed to the true wind speed, so the apparent wind increases to 40 knots, a whole gale and a different world.

The golden rules when running are:
- Get your speed and choice of sail right
- Keep your sails rigidly under control
- Steer with great care
- Never forget about the 'apparent wind factor'; this is the point of sailing where your judgement of wind speed is most vulnerable

SQUALLS

A squall approaching from astern

It is all too easy in an increasingly mechanised world to rely on a forecast and ignore the evidence of our own eyes. Squalls are mini-storms that move across the water. They may be self-contained or they may be part of a larger weather system, but it is always easy to see them coming in fair weather or foul.

AVOIDING A SQUALL

If all other considerations are equal, it is always worth dodging a squall if you can. You can 'plot' its approach just as you would a ship at sea and establish whether or not it is on a collision course. If both edges of the squall are changing their bearings in the same direction it is going to miss you. If one edge is opening one way and the other the opposite, then it is spreading its arms in welcome. Try a course alteration and see if it makes any difference. If it does you may be able to duck it successfully.

When a squall is rainy, it often makes a lovely radar target. Put the electronic bearing line on it and have another look in five minutes. If it's still on the line and getting closer, it's got your name on it.

ASSESSING A SQUALL

Generally, a squall takes the form of a heavy cloud. As a rule of thumb, if you can see the horizon underneath it then it will not be too severe. But if it has a full 'skirt' that is blotting out the horizon you are in for a soaking at the very least.

The big question is, will it produce wind or not? The answer is that at a distance you simply cannot tell by looking at it. I

The potential effects of a squall

once suffered a series of four apparently identical squalls one afternoon in the Caribbean. The first three brought only delicious cooling rain, and the fourth blew out my mainsail!

Squally weather occurs frequently along the cold front of a temperate depression, but squalls abound in tropical seas as well.

If there are boats between you and the squall watch them carefully. Are they falling over or sailing on unaffected?

When the squall is much closer you will be able to see if the wind is cutting up the water – but by then it may be too late. Be ready to go into one of your squall tactics.

Once the squall is upon you, you can place some reliance on the ancient saying:
When the rain's before the wind, tops'l sheets and halyards mind.
When the wind's before the rain, tops'ls soon you'll set again.

In other words, if the rain hits you before the wind does, watch out!

LINE SQUALLS

Line squalls can be found in any latitude although certain locations favour their formation. They are particularly popular, for example, in the Inter Tropical Convergence Zone, and also on the east coast of North America, where their movements are often forecast with a high degree of accuracy on the continuous weather bulletins broadcast on VHF.

They can be recognised by a long line of cloud advancing athwart the wind direction. Sometimes the cloud appears to be rolling over upon itself and frequently an arch-like phenomenon will be seen at the centre. You can sometimes discern the horizon under the cloud of a line squall, but in spite of this, it may produce winds of alarming ferocity. Beware of line squalls.

SQUALL TACTICS

If you suffer a sudden blow that you know will not last, there are three simple tactics for handling it without drama.

Shorten sail: Depending on your boat and your crew strength you may feel this is too much trouble, but it is very easy just to roll away the headsail. This simple reduction will be more than adequate to ride through most squalls.

Heave-to: Particularly if the wind is forward of the beam, heaving-to provides an easy way of reducing the strains produced by a passing squall. This is, of course, no use if you are sailing with a genoa as the spreaders may damage it as it lies aback. The boat will not balance properly either, so roll it away until there is no overlap with the mast and rigging. Full details of heaving to are in Chapter 8.

Run off: If you are laid over by a squall when reaching, the best solution is to run off square before the wind. This will not only reduce the apparent wind, it will also have the effect of bringing the boat upright once more. Do not think that because you are running with the wind you are necessarily increasing the time that you will be under the squall. The wind may not be blowing in the direction of the squall's advance, and even if it is, your boatspeed will not make a great deal of difference to the situation.

It is unusual for a squall to affect one boat for more than about 15 minutes, but so long as the boat is well handled, those 15 minutes will be very different from the shambles they could have been.

The anticipation of a squall will last for longer than the squall itself; use that time to prepare

Heaving-to can be a way of surviving a squall

5
NAVIGATION

Navigation can be defined as the art and science of directing the course of a vessel from one point to another in safety and in the shortest reasonable time. On a clear sunny day with a modern chart plotter up and running, the process presents no problems, but as the weather deteriorates, the job becomes somewhat more challenging.

In bad weather, sometimes everything happens at once. The chart plotter goes offline just at the boat falls off a wave and throws the almanac onto the cabin sole running with bilge water. The question of the boat's whereabouts can then degenerate into a nightmare lottery. With luck, you'll have a reliable secondary GPS system, perhaps on the smartphone or a tablet.

Without the main plotter, however, you may well still be down to paper chart navigation.

There aren't a lot of laughs attached to being an old-fashioned navigator in a gale, but before we look at some of the ways in which you can pace yourself and continue to produce the desired result, let's identify the enemy.

- Seasickness can turn every trip to the chart table into a gruelling and messy test of character. Even with the plotter still functioning it can still tempt you to do less than even the minimum of essential work.
- The motion of the boat and the general degree of wetness everywhere make meticulous chartwork almost impossible even for the most experienced navigator.
- Thick visibility can often put the cap on your joy. Even if visibility is not too bad, spotting buoys as both they and you ride up and down on different 15-foot waves is far from easy. It also becomes difficult to count the time sequences of lights.
- Estimating leeway is almost impossible as your boat is hurled around by the seas, but you can be sure it is greater than you think. I once made 15 degrees on a run down the North Sea from Norway with a gale of wind on the beam.
- Distance logs can become erratic as a light hull leaps from wave-top to

wave-top. Many an impeller ends up measuring enough air speed to render the record of 'distance run' a nonsense. Your best bet is an old-fashioned heavy trailing log with a long line, but these have long since been consigned to history or Grandad's garage.
- The course steered is unlikely to be very close to the course you ordered up and the damping of even the best hand-bearing compass is not enough to ensure a clear bearing in a very rough sea.

All these delights, together with others too numerous to mention, do not militate in favour of nit-picking chartwork. Instead, you need to make a realistic assessment of the degree of accuracy you can hope for and plan your course accordingly. Make sure to allow for deterioration in your personal performance or you may demand more of yourself than you have to give and end up by submitting to seasickness and exhaustion.

The lines which you draw, both physically and metaphorically, between danger and safety must be a lot further from the edge of disaster than you might choose on a calm day. Because every part of your operation is less accurate you need to leave a greater margin for not being where you hope you might be.

Instead of a course line being the width of a pencil point, you should at least consider that it may have become a tight cone spreading out from your point of departure. The angle of the root of the cone is likely the helming error. If the cone brushes too close to a danger you should adjust the course required accordingly. Should that set the cone into danger on the other side, then you'll have to keep a particularly sharp look out, go somewhere else, or fire the helmsman.

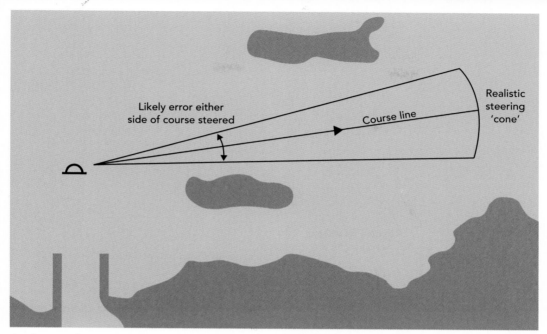

As the weather gets worse, your navigational accuracy will deteriorate too; you should convert all your course lines to 'cones' and take care to keep them well clear of dangers such as lee shores

Should you find yourself having to work up an Estimated Position (EP) the same issues apply, but bear in mind that the gale may also be affecting the tide strength and direction. The tide vector will become less positive and instead of an EP there will be an estimated area of position. As always, assume you are in the corner of the area nearest to danger, before deciding where to go next.

Position fixing is often a shaky procedure in heavy weather. Use transits wherever possible as a source of position lines. They are always accurate, quick to observe and easy to plot. Compass bearings may be wildly inaccurate, and you should spare yourself those sick-making sessions squinting through a compass prism by using the ship herself and the steering compass whenever possible. If your mark is nearly ahead, or astern, steer directly for it (or away from it) for a few seconds and read the ship's heading. This

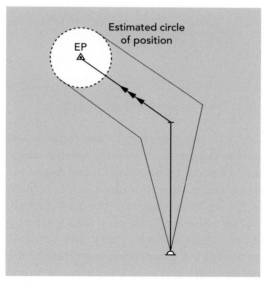

Reduced accuracy means that an EP has to be inflated into an estimated area of position

is a particularly useful method of checking whether or not you are the right side of a clearing line if you are skirting an area of danger.

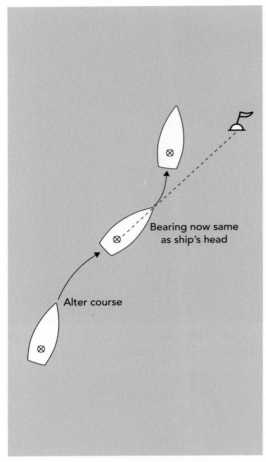

Using the boat as a bearing compass

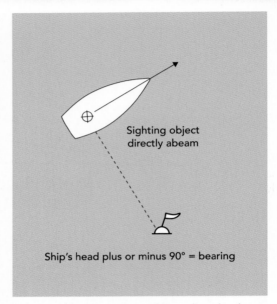

Sighting object directly abeam

Ship's head plus or minus 90° = bearing

Taking a bearing on an object directly abeam using the ship's compass

ORGANISATION

Even if everything is operating as it should, when you know the weather is going to get rough, do as much planning as you can before the boat starts leaping about. You can calculate in advance tidal heights for port entry, stream vectors, critical bearings, off-lying dangers and any amount of other details while you still feel like a spring lamb. If you leave such work until you're sick and tired of the whole business, it is only too easy either not to bother at all or to make a dangerous mistake through sheer fatigue.

Tidiness at the chart table really pays dividends in rough weather. Have more than one chart out at once and they will surely jump the fiddle into the puddle under the companionway. You won't have time in your brief visits to the 'office' to search for pencils and plotters. They must be where they always are. I keep my pencil in the working page of the logbook; the book is then closed – and hence impervious to drips – and the pencil is where I want it. Dividers can pin the cook to the galley

Don't forget that if you have radar, it will always deliver a completely reliable range and bearing to anything it can see. One inestimable benefit of radar in this context is that it emanates from the boat herself, not some external source. If GPS should go down for any reason, radar will continue to deliver the goods. Relate its data to the paper chart and you should be in prime shape.

You can get a reliable bearing on an object by sighting it directly abeam down the mainsheet traveller, or anything else that runs athwartships. Add or subtract 90 degrees from the ship's heading and you have its rough bearing.

very effectively if the boat throws them properly, so don't give them the chance. Drill a hole in one corner of the chart table and keep your dividers plugged into it.

SOME FINAL POINTS

The pious hope of us all is, of course, that the electronics won't go bust and that we can continue to rely on them. Electronic chart plotters are an absolute godsend in heavy weather. If you don't have one, at least download an app such as Navionics onto your smartphone. The cost is ludicrously small and the safety it offers might prove priceless.

I'm not suggesting that such a device can be a substitute for a bigger screen, but when used in conjunction with a paper chart to supply the big picture it still offers a package for which navigators of half a century ago would have sold their souls. Not to have one is crazy. In fact, even if you use a full bulkhead plotter with up-to-date charts installed it's still worth keeping a tiny app as a backup independent of the ship's systems.

Regardless of the size or sophistication of your plotter, be sure that the 'projected track' vector is switched on and cannot be confused with a heading vector. Knowing where you are actually going at a given moment is of far greater value than having confirmation of what your compass can tell you for free. Projected track can be given various names by different manufacturers, but whatever it is called, its value cannot be overestimated as you watch its long wavering finger point across the electronic chart, telling you most of what you need to know at a glance.

It pays now to keep your navigation as simple as possible. Stay healthy, stay on deck where the action is, or rest yourself in the bunk for when you will be needed, but whatever else you do or don't do, keep the paper logbook up to date. If the electronics should fail for any reason, the last known position, the log reading and the time you plotted it, remain the lifeline they have always been.

Whatever happens, keep the logbook up to date

6
STRATEGY, TACTICS & THE WEATHER

Unless you are the sort of person who goes out looking for trouble, avoidance of heavy weather has to be better than risking direct involvement. At one end of the scale, this might mean being on the opposite side of the world to miss a hurricane season. At the other, it can be simply making a temporary course alteration to steer around the worst of a squall, but if you are not in a position to keep clear of a forecast blow, prudent action based on a shrewd assessment of developments should see you through.

You will be using all the available data to try to stay one step ahead of the weather. Nowadays the information we need can be drawn from many sources. The natural ones have been used since Noah looked heavenwards on the Fortieth Day of the flood and launched his pigeons. Later, reading the sky and the sea state was assisted by the barometer. Then came radio, but even this brought the UK only the Shipping and Inshore Forecasts, augmented by long-range bulletins for those blessed with short-wave receivers. Now, the internet has taken up the slack and offers an endless selection of forecasts,

some of them reaching a week or more ahead. The difference is dramatic, but none of them is worth the candle unless the information they supply is interpreted with wisdom and acted upon positively.

THE WEATHER FORECAST

Armed with a suitable forecast and the ability to interpret it, any sailor should be halfway to avoiding trouble, but as is often the case, it isn't always that simple. It's a bit like an echo sounder. In the hands of a novice it does no more than advise how deep the water is at a particular time and place. To an expert it can provide the key to a whole world of knowledge.

However excellent the data and predictions from the outside world may be, what counts in the end is what is happening to your ship right now, and what you deduce is going to happen in the hours to come.

Weather forecasting may be official and professional or you may do it yourself by observing barometer, sky, wind, precipitation, wave pattern, visibility, temperature and whether or not your rheumatism is playing up. Both types of prediction are of great importance.

FORECASTS FOR COASTAL WATERS

While internet forecasting has taken over as most people's primary source of weather data, radio forecasts remain important. In Britain the BBC do a wonderful job by broadcasting a synopsis and forecast four times a day. With the right equipment you can receive Long Wave Radio 4 from the Azores almost to the Arctic Circle so, within those limits, anyone who understands English can be informed, at least about the coming 24 hours. In the United States the meteorological channels on VHF broadcast continuously, giving the synopsis and local forecasts for the adjacent coastal waters.

Sea areas are big places, however, and local conditions can be expected to vary from the general forecast. Most countries issue excellent inshore waters forecasts by radio to cope with this. Times and frequencies of these are published in the Nautical Almanacs but if you don't speak the local language, you may find the information less than helpful unless you are well prepared.

To understand a foreign shipping forecast, you need to be able to count from one to ten in the language concerned, and you need to be able to recognise a few vital words. Choose a yachtsman's pilot book for your cruise area which contains a good glossary. Never mind a translation of 'cucumber', what about 'southwest gale'? If you have studied the form of the foreign forecast and are aware of the boundaries of the sea areas to which it refers, its message will be clear enough.

While you are within range of coastal radio stations it is always worth keeping your VHF radio switched on in heavy weather. It will keep you abreast of any navigational warnings, and in the UK important weather information is given out as soon as it is issued by the Meteorological Office. Gale warnings are repeated, new gale warnings are reported and, if you have missed a BBC forecast, the salient features will be given out again in due course.

Your first sign of an approaching blow is likely to be a gale warning. This may not be for you, but for sea areas between you and an approaching weather system. By using the synopsis to predict what is likely to happen, and checking this against the reports of coastal radio stations, you may get up to 24 hours' notice of a gale coming your way

All this, however, is somewhat pedestrian when compared with developments such as Navtex and the internet. Within reach of 4 and 5G coverage, the internet runs rings around Navtex. There are so many good internet marine forecasts available either free or at minimal cost that every sailor seems have their own favourite, but the bedrock of any onboard forecast must remain the surface pressure chart or what I prefer to call the synoptic chart. These are available for the North Atlantic from the UK Met Office website. Knowing how to read this and noting the five-day prognosis makes sense of all the arrow-driven internet forecasts and puts things in a proper perspective.

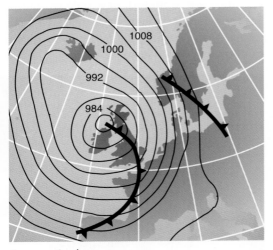

A synoptic chart

The reliability of the seven-day forecasts with wind arrows, rain, sea state and visibility gets better every year. At the time of writing (2023) it is fair to say that 24 hours is likely to be spot-on, 48 nearly so, 72 probably, with a steady deterioration of certainty thereafter. Some of these forecasts can be fine-tuned to remarkably tight local conditions, which certainly cannot be said for Navtex forecasts which use large sea areas. However, Navtex can be received hundreds of miles offshore, far beyond the range of the telephone and it stores its forecasts. It can be left on while a boat is in commission so there's always the latest forecast when you have time to look at it. If you have enough money and intend making passages outside ordinary internet coverage but still within Navtex range, Navtex may well be worth the investment. Along the coast, it probably isn't any more.

A sky like this, a falling barometer and a backing and strengthening wind add up to bad news. Add a heavy swell coming with the wind and things are starting to look interesting. If the barometer is falling at a rate of 6mb or more in three hours then hang on to your hat, for this is a guarantee of winds approaching gale force

OCEAN FORECASTING

The difference between ocean sailing and coastal is that within even a hundred miles of shelter, given modern forecasting, there is every chance of avoiding the worst of what's to come. In mid-ocean, unless you have a very fast boat, no amount of internet know-how and downloaded files can supply a life-long 'get-out-of-jail-free' card. Sooner or later, we're all going to get hit.

Fortunately, while mid-ocean gales are often stronger than those experienced around land masses with higher seas to match, they are rarely as dangerous because there is nothing to run into out there. The chances of foundering in deep water are far less than the possibility of a terminal encounter with the rocks, cliffs, tide rips and lee shores of coastal waters. That said, the realistic availability and quality of global forecasting accessible to ocean sailors is wonderful to me, who began cruising before any internet or satellite communications.

AVAILABLE SOURCES

Full internet, albeit at slower-than-terrestrial speeds and at great expense, can be delivered to any yacht whose owner has deep enough pockets. The rest of us who want to keep abreast of what weather is coming our way can manage perfectly well with more modest arrangements. Any onboard set-up that can provide email is capable of downloading a synoptic chart. It can back this up with so-called GRIB files via email. These offer all you want in terms of data and can be downloaded onto an electronic chart. Add in the time-honoured methods of monitoring the barometer, the sky and the run of the sea and you have everything that's needed to forecast and, if possible, avoid heavy weather. The only question to be answered is how to access this information.

This is generally achieved by means of a satellite phone, perhaps an Iridium, or long-range radio via SSB (single side-band) enhanced with a pactor modem.

A full analysis of SSB radio with its benefits and apparent complexities versus a simple satellite phone hooked up to a PC lies beyond the scope of this work, but for guidance, the following may help:

The plus points of SSB
- Long-range distress broadcasting
- No online charges for emails, position reports, etc. but emails need to be short
- Worldwide availability of GRIB weather forecasts, weather reports and weather faxes
- Allows access to broadcast 'nets' among cruising boats. These are used to share information, calls for technical assistance and, in particular, gossip which is always a favourite
- Scheduled communications with buddy boats

Downsides of SSB
- Cost of installation and general workload of assembling the kit. A whip aerial or insulated backstay and ground plate are minimum requirements. This must all be carefully installed for successful reception and transmission. There is no room for compromise
- UK users require a long-range radio certificate, although a lifetime Restricted Radiotelephone Operator's permit (VHF DSC) and a 10-year ship's radio licence for the SSB are acceptable. Do not confuse this with a full-on HAM radio licence which is rigorously tested

Plus points of Satphones
- Easy to install via 12-volt charging units and USB laptop connections

- Although by no means cheap, the hardware is relatively inexpensive. An additional external antenna can be worth its weight in gold
- As easy to use as a mobile phone
- No online charges for short emails, position reports, etc.
- GRIB weather forecasts, weather reports and weather faxes can be received worldwide
- Private phone calls can be made anywhere, so long as you don't mind the cost

Downsides of satphones
- Can be even slower than SSB for emailing, etc.
- All internet time must be paid for either by contract or more expensive off-contract payments
- No cruiser net availability, so if you enjoy feeling you are part of a community, this will cut you off
- Faster, more powerful internet connections are available with large dish or dome antennae, but these are a lot more money

TACTICS & STRATEGY

LONG-TERM & OCEAN STRATEGY

The best definition of seamanship I know is that it is the art of staying out of trouble. Successful heavy weather strategy is just the same. It is, quite simply, the question of being in the right place at the right time.

The official and unofficial pilot books for all the oceans give the general tendencies for wind and wave as the seasons change. *World Cruising Routes* by Jimmy Cornell, *Ocean Passages for the World* (UKHO) and, of course, accounts by sailors who have been there before can all be considered. 'Routeing charts' compiled on a monthly basis from data supplied by ships since the 19th century are still produced in the UK and the US and remain of primary value.

No skipper with a choice in the matter and nothing to prove would ever think of crossing the North Atlantic in winter. Anyone who does and makes it in one piece survives only as proof of the Everlasting Mercy. All published opinion on the subject advises strongly against rounding Cape Horn between April and November while any sailors sufficiently deaf to the experience of ages to attempt a tradewind crossing from Europe to the Caribbean in August will have only themselves to blame for a slow passage, a bloody nose, or, if they cannot avoid the ever-increasing likelihood of a full-blown hurricane, maybe even a one-way ticket to Davy Jones' Locker.

Strategy won't guarantee you an easy ride. If you have to cross any ocean north or south of 35 degrees you may be served up a gale to sharpen your wits even in high summer, but if you stick within the limits imposed by a mature appraisal of world weather patterns, you are giving yourself the best chance of not meeting something you can't handle.

Such questions are all matters of long-term strategy. For those engaged on shorter trips, strategy is still important, but on a smaller scale.

INSHORE TACTICS

Heavy weather tactics break down into two areas: open-water storm survival techniques and handling bad conditions in closer proximity to land. The former are considered in Chapter 8. Before considering specific tactics where land may be involved, two vital areas of concern must be understood. These are the lee shore and the dangers of misinterpreting the apparent wind.

THE LEE SHORE

If strategy has failed, and you run into the heavy weather you were hoping to avoid, the first priority is not to come into contact with anything more solid than the wind or the waves.

The danger to be averted at all costs is that of letting yourself be placed in a perilous position from which your boat does not have the sail and / or engine power to extricate herself. It isn't usually the sea that causes the real trouble, it's land. More specifically, it's being blown onto a 'lee shore'.

Back in the day, outward bound square riggers used not to turn south from the English Channel until they were several degrees west of the Biscay capes of Ushant and Finisterre. With modern yachts and today's forecasting this may be a bit excessive, but the point is well made nonetheless.

In heavy weather, keeping well clear of any potential lee shore is 'Priority Number One'. The only complete answer to this is not to go anywhere near one in the first place.

However, there will be times – perhaps when approaching a harbour of refuge – when a calculated risk is worth taking, especially for a yacht powerful enough to sail out of danger.

A place may not look too bad with the yacht in good order, but if she were to be disabled – typically by an engine failure – it can take on a horribly different aspect. Perhaps it's because I spent so much of my youth disappointed by unreliable engines that whenever I'm motoring to windward of a nasty obstruction, I'm never happy until well clear. I'm also constantly working out contingency plans for what to do if the

fuel filters clog in the rough water, or a sea across the deck carries a stray rope into the propeller.

TRUE & APPARENT WIND: THE DANGERS OF MISINTERPRETING THE BREEZE

Six knots boatspeed downwind calms a 30-knot near-gale into a 24-knot stiff breeze. Upwind, the same blow is ratcheted up to 36 knots – a whole gale. Pressure on the sail, which is a multiple of wind speed, is virtually doubled, so any plan involving a major course change in hard winds should bear this firmly in mind. Even where you intend ploughing straight on, an emergency can find you out, so the best advice is not to risk a fright by running downwind over-canvassed and always to be aware of the true wind speed.

With all stresses so much eased by running off, the manoeuvre is great for dealing with minor crises. When a roller headsail gear snags, for example, anyone trained in dinghies turns automatically into the wind to let everything flap. This is because the dinghy's first priority is not to capsize. A keelboat won't tip over and a flogging sail is a major hazard. Luffing up can turn a nuisance into a disaster.

Running off, if sea room allows it, defuses the situation. The main can then blanket the wind from the foredeck and transform working up there into a relative pleasure.

Running off

TACTICAL OPTIONS WITH LAND A FACTOR

The obvious advice if a bad blow seems at all likely is to stay in port if possible. If it's a case of, 'Man, you gotta go,' make sure the passage plan is safely clear of potential danger, makes proper consideration of any tidal effects on the sea state and gives due weight to ports of refuge. At least then you know what to expect and will have a sort of 'set-piece' situation.

Sometimes you've just got to go – in this case, coming out of Bembridge in a force 9 gale

Being caught at sea is a different matter. Any decision out there will be governed by the wind direction in relation to where you'd like to go, or any viable alternatives. The state of the crew, sea room and dangerous areas such as tide rips will also be factors.

Here are some typical choices:

1. CARRY ON REGARDLESS

If you reckon you can do it, it's often best to bite the bullet, batten down the hatches, brief the hands that this is not going to be fun, then slug it out. When your destination is distant, and especially if it lies to leeward and you have plenty of sea room, you may well feel that whatever this blow may send, it isn't going to affect your progress in any way other than to make you wet, cold and miserable. Just make sure that you have taken all the precautions discussed in Chapter 2 to make your boat watertight and ready for a bouncing.

Switch to your heavy weather watch routine. Bend on storm canvas in good time. Stoke up the five-day stew, make sure the baby is sympathetically stowed, and keep on yachting.

If you carry on regardless, you might come out the other side smiling

2. GO INTO SURVIVAL MODE OUT AT SEA

If the strength of the gale is such, or likely to become such, that carrying on is out of the question for your boat, when there is no reachable shelter to windward and no safe shelter to leeward, you have no choice but to ride it out at sea.

This is never a popular decision. No-one enjoys 24 hours of being stood on his or her head under an icy firehose of abrasive seawater. But if you make it clear to the crew that the alternative may well be even less savoury, they usually back you up in the end. Swimming in 25-foot breakers holds little appeal, even for the most seasick sailors.

Sometimes you have to go into survival mode

Unless a knock-down seems likely, the boat isn't going to be in immediate danger from the water itself, but the nearest lee shore could finish her off. A summer gale probably won't blow for more than 24 hours at the most, so employing survival tactics in the open may be the safest option.

As mentioned above, the tactics you may choose to adopt for riding out the gale are discussed in Chapter 8 but, whatever you decide, you will require all the sea room you can get. If there is a choice, work out which shore is going to be the dangerous one and then use all available means to place yourself as distant from it as conditions allow.

Once you are confident that you are far enough off you can jog to windward, heave-to or even lie a'hull if you have to, but until you have plenty of sea room you can never afford to relax.

3. GO & HIDE SOMEWHERE

If you don't fancy carrying on and shelter can safely be reached, this is the obvious answer. However, a harbour entrance that's friendly on a fine summer's day may be a death-trap in different conditions. Here are the points for selecting a bolt-hole:

- **Downwind:** Running for shelter is generally less stressful for the crew than beating up to weather. It's also easier on the boat. You can't escape the fact, however, that the coast you're approaching is potentially dangerous.
- **Upwind:** In even a near-gale, it's going to be tough smashing your way to shelter upwind. The good news is that, as the coast approaches, the waves smooth out and the going gets easier. The bottom line states that almost any refuge lying to windward with a sheltering shoreline behind it can be entered safely. The problem is getting 'up' there in the first place.

ASSESSING PORTS IN A STORM

A harbour on a lee shore must have an unambiguous entrance broad enough to remove worries about controlling the boat as you run in. Any sudden shoaling will pile up the seas. If a narrow entrance is tidal, will the stream be slack, flooding or ebbing? If it's ripping out over a bar against a gale, the seas will become dangerous, especially if they're whipped up by bounce-back from piers or walls. And how about any turns to be made inside?

I once ran for shelter into a river that swung immediately to windward inside the entrance. I came in OK, but when I got out of the waves and steered the boat up into the breeze, she wasn't powerful enough to face it and I was left running back out to sea with my tail between my legs.

The factors go on and on. The trick is to be coldly objective and not to make pretty mental images about a fantasy which may prove at odds with the reality.

All-weather harbours are rare wonders, but to the sailor on the edge they are the breath of life.

One thing is sure about going for any shelter, anywhere: when dirty weather is in the offing, follow the advice of Lord Nelson and 'Lose not a moment'. Reefing too soon when driving for shelter could rob you of the extra knot of speed to reach safety before the first 60-knot squall.

Give the boat her head and use the engine if need be; in the end it may pay handsomely.

Think before you run for a harbour mouth in a heavy breeze. It may look like this when you get there. If there are no other options, you would be well advised to ride out the gale at sea

7

BOAT PERFORMANCE

Before it is possible to evaluate potential storm survival tactics, it is critical to understand the probable plus and minus points of the type of yacht being sailed. That is why this chapter appears here in the book.

When we are talking about the 'performance' of a motor car we tend to think in terms of its acceleration, top speed and road holding. You might say something similar about a sailing boat, but this would miss a vital point. There are aspects of their performance, irrelevant on a normal yachting day, which become immensely important when facing difficult conditions.

To say that any yacht must be a compromise is one of the clichés of the sport, but it remains perfectly true. The problem lies in deciding not whether, but what, you are prepared to compromise:

- High performance in wind strengths under force 3 perhaps, or your personal safety in an open-sea gale?
- A bit of extra internal volume, or the ability to heave-to?
- Five degrees of pointing to windward in calm water, or the capacity to go straight with a lashed helm for long enough to let you have a comfortable brew?

Boats vary so much that in order to discuss how to set about surviving a bad blow it is vital to look at some of their characteristics, and the way these may affect the skipper's options.

THREE TYPES FOR COMPARISON

Sailing boat design has developed down so many avenues that it is impossible to deal with them all in this book. The question of multihull seaworthiness, for example, lies outside my personal experience. Another sizeable group not represented here is that of twin bilge keel yachts, but if you own one of these useful cruising boats you should be able to draw your own conclusions from the information that follows.

The types to be studied are:

- **Boat A:** A long-keeled, heavy displacement yacht with the rudder attached to the trailing edge of the keel
- **Boat B:** A modern yacht with a longish fin keel, often with encapsulated ballast and a rudder at least partially supported by a skeg
- **Boat C:** A relatively light, beamy, flat-bottomed yacht with a deep fin keel and a spade rudder supported only by its own shaft

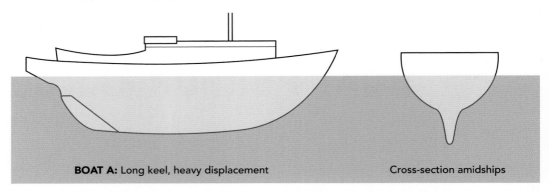

BOAT A: Long keel, heavy displacement   Cross-section amidships

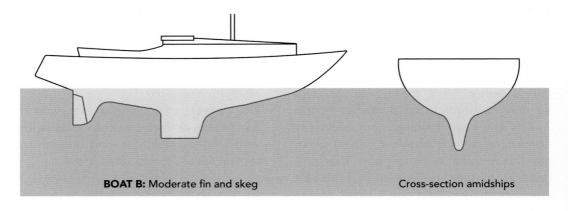

BOAT B: Moderate fin and skeg   Cross-section amidships

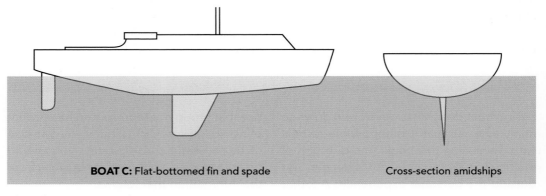

BOAT C: Flat-bottomed fin and spade   Cross-section amidships

Three boats compared

Because this is a book about heavy weather sailing, we are only going to look at features of the boats which directly affect their hard weather performance. The relevance may be slight or even reversed when sailing in good, or even moderately poor conditions. Since most of us spend the majority of our sailing lives successfully avoiding a reckoning with the Great Examiner, the designers of many modern production boats are able to ignore some serious shortcomings in the ultimate ability of their products.

In case that sounds like a mere statement of opinion, let's examine some of the general elements that help a boat deal effectively with dreadful weather and be specific about how well endowed with these qualities each of our three yachts may be.

WORKING TO WINDWARD

Boat A: Probably not as close-winded as the other two owing to her less dynamically efficient keel shape and the fact that her rig may well be of a lower aspect ratio. These will not stop her getting to windward, but she will need to be sailed freer than the others. She should be a powerful sail carrier, but she is going to give her crew a wet ride.

Boat B: A great windward performer in a blow. Close-winded, powerful and quick enough on the helm to steer over each wave if you need to. Faster to windward than Boat A, and sometimes even wetter in consequence.

Boat C: Because she is relatively light, this boat needs less canvas than the others to drive her, which is a useful feature. Rig and keel are highly efficient, so she points and foots well, but she needs careful steering. A moment's inattention and she slams into the trough, waking the sleepers even if they are feigning death, and effectively stopping her. On account of her high degree of buoyancy and large freeboard she should be the driest of the three.

DIRECTIONAL STABILITY

A boat that dances and yaws perpetually about her course is tiring for those steering her. They are thus more apt to make serious mistakes when running. Even if they manage to avoid errors, morale will be sapped, and they become exhausted earlier than they otherwise would.

Boat A: A joy to steer. A long keel and plenty of draught well aft keep her moving straight and true. If she rolls or heels, her easy sections will cause no serious change in helm balance.

Boat B: Much quicker on the helm than Boat A. She will be simple enough to steer with the wind forward of the beam and, as it moves aft, the rudder at the aft extremity makes for a long lever arm and effective steering. So long as the keel is moulded into the hull rather than bolted onto a flat section, her shape is sufficiently natural to enable her to maintain a reasonable balance if she heels hard in a gust.

Boat C: This boat has little natural directional stability, relying mainly on her large spade rudder to keep her going in the right direction. Her wide beam and flat floor tend to induce changing helm balance when the boat rolls or heels, which means that anyone steering in big waves must work constantly to maintain course, especially with the wind abaft the beam. Often it is impossible for the helmsman to leave the wheel long enough to attend to a headsail sheet.

The helm balance, which may well be beautiful in steady conditions, is likely to suddenly fly out of order because, if the

Boat A beating to windward

Boat B beating to windward

Boat C beating to windward

boat heels beyond the normal angle, her tortured sections cause an eccentric boat shape to be immersed. It is by no means unknown for such a boat to broach-tack herself against the helmsman's best efforts.

This poor directional stability also means that it is necessary to maintain the right sail combination with the wind forward of the beam. Too much sail and you have a mad bull on your hands, kept on the rails in gusty conditions only by playing the mainsheet. Not enough and the boat is stopped by the seas, because with her light weight she has little momentum to carry her through. A

boat of type A or B can be harder pressed without drastic results.

All of this may be of no concern to a full racing crew in Boat C, prepared to work hard and constantly enjoy the benefits the potential performance offers. In a short-handed cruising yacht, it can be a trial.

STRUCTURAL STRENGTH

Hull, rudder and rig must not fail. In the end, success depends on the boat being well found. Generally, a heavier boat will have an easier motion and probably a heavier, stronger rig and fittings.

Boats A and B have properly supported rudders. If Boat C were to fall backwards off a wave with her rudder hard over, the shaft would need to be exceedingly strong to guarantee avoiding damage. There is no doubt that such rudders are unnecessarily vulnerable.

STATIC LATERAL RESISTANCE

When a hull is moving well through the water its lateral resistance depends upon the efficiency of its keel and the rest of its immersed body. It is not necessarily related to its total immersed area. A modern deep-keeled yacht of type C develops more hydrodynamic 'lift' from the keel than the heavy displacement type A. So long as it has positive forward motion, its dynamic lateral resistance may be greater.

Unfortunately, in storm conditions the time will come when you may ask the boat to stop rather than go – to heave to for example (see Chapter 8). The situation is then reversed. Once it is stationary a hull's resistance to drift is largely proportionate to its immersed lateral area. Accordingly, Boat A has enormous static lateral resistance and is in with a good chance of being able to weather a moderate gale by heaving to. Boat C has hardly any static resistance at all. Boat B falls in between.

Yachts of type C generally have a high freeboard and therefore a lot of windage in addition to low values for static lateral resistance. Their ability to go sideways once the keel has stalled is therefore considerable. This feature also affects handling under power at low speed in harbours in the sort of vicious crosswinds to be expected when sheltering from storms.

Boat A is well mannered and steady but not particularly manoeuvrable. She is often a nightmare to steer astern. Boat B behaves herself on both counts. C is exceptionally manoeuvrable when under way ahead or astern but is liable to embarrass you by blowing sideways if you give her a chance by stopping.

MOTION

A lively motion will rapidly wear out all hands, leading to accidents, bad decisions, lethargy and a multiplication of sorrows.

Boat A will have an easy motion because her weight and consequent inertia resist the effect of every passing wavelet. Her gentle sections will assist and so will the fact that her mass is comparatively evenly distributed.

Boat C, with her light weight, flat bottom, low inertia and concentrated ballast will show a marked tendency to throw sleepers from their bunks, sailors off the deck, cooks into the soup and everyone into a tired, irritable humour.

Boat B lies somewhere between the two.

'PUMPABILITY'

Any boat is capable of accidental flooding or, at least, of taking in too much water for comfort in a bad gale. If her pumps are to stand a chance of clearing her, a boat must have a deep bilge for the water to drain into.

Boat A has an enormous capacity to keep unwanted water below the cabin sole. Furthermore, since the water can pass straight into the bilge it will probably remain clean of debris and less likely to clog the pump strum boxes. Water has to be present in colossal quantities before it encroaches on the accommodation, food lockers, batteries and all the other items you would prefer to keep dry, and since the pump inlet is well down in the keel it should never come to this.

Boat B may well have an adequately deep bilge space. Some do, some don't.

Boat C may have virtually no bilge at all. The only way to keep your lockers dry on such a vessel is to sponge out the bilge, as the floor of the boat is so flat that a two-inch pump suction cannot get a grip on the bilge water until there is sufficient to invade the accommodation.

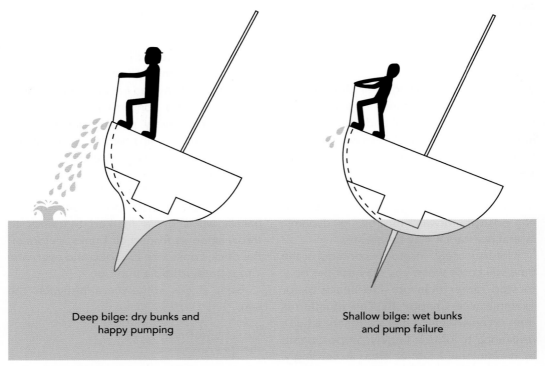

Deep bilge: dry bunks and
happy pumping

Shallow bilge: wet bunks
and pump failure

A flat-floored boat with no real bilge cannot be pumped out, and will soak her accommodation

HELMING POSITION

All boats, whatever their type, must have a steering position that is comfortable and secure. This means that the cockpit should be deep and low down in the boat. It is not insignificant that over a century ago all Bristol Channel sailing pilot cutters had deep, self-draining cockpits sited right aft. These boats were conceived by men of vast experience to be safe at sea. Walk-through accommodation, aft staterooms big enough for a serious party, and other such considerations came nowhere in their planning. They were concerned only with producing the most seaworthy arrangement possible, and they knew what they were doing.

Many modern yachts have excellent cockpits the pilots would have enjoyed. A centre cockpit in all but the largest yachts is generally high from the water to allow for the walk-through arrangements in the accommodation. This makes it inherently less safe as the motion up there is liable to be worse. Another reason why the working boat cockpits were right aft was to keep the crew as far away from the action as possible. If you have any doubts about this, try sitting in an aft cockpit for ten minutes or so on a lively day, then go up to the foredeck. The difference is dramatic.

This fine sea-going cockpit is history, but you get the idea ...

A very open and shallow cockpit which might be a dangerous place to linger in a big sea

CAPACITY TO ANCHOR SUCCESSFULLY

Anchoring may be the last card in your hand that will save you from stranding, but even if you are merely riding out a gale in a sheltered anchorage you need a well-mannered boat if you do not want to be up half the night dragging, or in fear of dragging.

Boat A, because of her substantial inertia and static lateral resistance, will not sheer about a great deal when lying to anchor. Her comparatively deep forefoot will help as well. Furthermore, since she is heavy, carrying the extra weight of plenty of good ground tackle will not be a problem for her – so she has no excuse for not being suitably equipped. Also, her low freeboard will keep down her hull windage. All of which give her anchors the best chance of holding firm.

Boat B has less forefoot and is lighter for her length, so she will not lie so quietly.

Boat C, having no appreciable forefoot in the water, will allow her head to blow off with every gust of wind. She will sail around shamelessly, snubbing her anchor at the end of each surge. Even if she doesn't pull it out, her ill-mannered behaviour will not encourage confident slumber.

STABILITY

Given that the skipper has arranged to keep his boat well clear of shore-related dangers, by far the greatest evil that can befall her out at sea is to be knocked down onto her beam ends, or even completely capsized. For our purposes we can think of stability as the boat's ability to resist these horrors or, if she should succumb, her power to get back on her feet as quickly as possible.

Heavy weather stability can be considered at two levels: static and dynamic.

STATIC STABILITY

This is the calculated power of a boat to resist a capsizing force applied steadily, in theoretical conditions. The results by no means tell the whole story. They are, however, a good starting point.

Illustrated is a 'GZ' curve, which is a graph of the increase or decrease in a boat's 'righting arm' with changing angles of heel. The righting arm is the lateral distance between the centre of gravity and the centre of buoyancy. Depending upon the relative positions of the two centres, and how the centre of buoyancy moves with the angle of heel, the boat will, at some stage, become negatively stable, which means that she will be perfectly happy to float upside down.

The two GZ curves plotted here are based on the official report on the disastrous 1979 Fastnet Race which saw a large number of race boats unable to handle a major storm south of Ireland. Little has changed since then. One is for a 32-foot cruiser-racer similar to our Boat B.

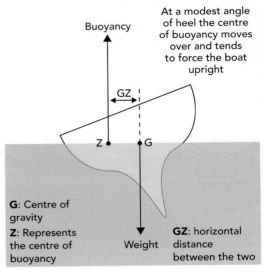

At a modest angle of heel the centre of buoyancy moves over and tends to force the boat upright

Buoyancy

GZ

Z   G

G: Centre of gravity

Z: Represents the centre of buoyancy

Weight

GZ: horizontal distance between the two

The GZ curve plots the distance between the centre of buoyancy and the centre of gravity at increasing angles of heel

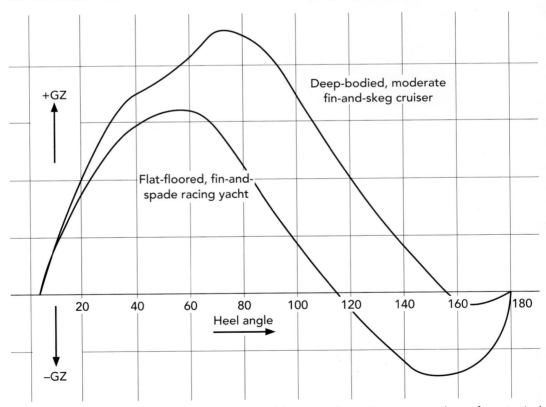

Deep-bodied, moderate fin-and-skeg cruiser

+GZ

Flat-floored, fin-and-spade racing yacht

20   40   60   80   100   120   140   160   180

Heel angle

–GZ

Two GZ curves – one for a Contessa 32, a notably seaworthy cruiser-racer, and one for a typical flat-floored yacht

The other is for an out-and-out racing boat of similar length overall, displaying many characteristics copied in beamy modern cruisers of type C. You will notice that boat B is extremely stable at 80 degrees of heel (virtually on her beam ends) while the flat-bottomed beamy racer is already losing stability from 55 degrees onwards.

Look at the situation at 90 degrees of heel. The righting arm of Boat B is more than double that of the flat-floored yacht, which means that not only will she be trying twice as hard to pull herself vertical again if she is laid flat, but also that she will try twice as hard not to be pushed over in the first place.

The racing boat becomes negatively stable at about 115 degrees while our heroine fights it out right up to 155 degrees. Even then, she is only marginally stable upside-down. Any passing wave would knock her back into a positively stable state. In contrast the flat-floored yacht is remarkably stable once well and truly inverted. Such craft are on record as having remained thus for minutes on end following a capsize at sea.

The heavy displacement yacht of type A has a centre of gravity which is higher than that of a fin-and-skeg cruiser-racer and her static stability will probably fall somewhere between that of the two types discussed.

DYNAMIC STABILITY

When it comes to real life situations, a yacht is not hove down by a steady force: she is knocked over by wave action. Part of her capacity to resist knockdowns is expressed by the GZ curve, but other factors are of even greater importance.

Following the 1979 Fastnet Race, the Society of Naval Architects and Marine Engineers (SNAME) and the United States Yacht Racing Union (USYRU) produced a report which defined the factors which

enable a yacht to resist being capsized by a breaking wave. In order to do this they drew on existing data and also commissioned a series of carefully controlled experiments.

The results of their work show that the factors which contribute most to a vessel's resistance to capsize are displacement and roll moment of inertia.

When a boat capsizes, she rolls over. Rolling is a form of motion and, like any other motion, before it can get underway, it must first overcome the forces of inertia. 'Roll moment of inertia' is a convenient way of expressing the amount of inertia to be overcome before a boat begins to roll over convincingly.

The vertical position of the centre of gravity makes surprisingly little theoretical difference, though the report says that in practice 'low positions resist capsize and help assure recovery from upside-down stable equilibrium.'

The elements that make up a boat's total displacement can be expressed in terms of their relative weight by this diagram for a typical yacht:

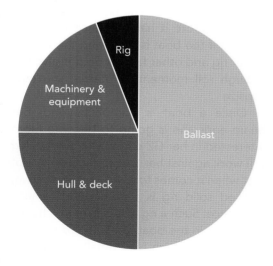

If we now express the same elements in the proportion that they affect roll moment of inertia the diagram looks like this:

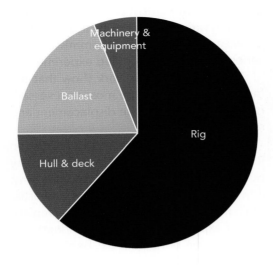

The message is clear. Contrary to what one might expect, when it comes to being capsized by a breaking wave the effect of a heavy rig is beneficial. This is because of its inertia, or its initial resistance to movement. If you hold the boat on her beam ends, a heavy rig will have a bad effect upon her GZ curve, but this is not what happens at sea. A wave hits the boat and passes on. If the boat's displacement and roll moment of inertia are sufficient to resist it, it will pass on before it has a chance to flatten her. But if the boat is light, and the weight of her rig and other factors do not give her enough roll moment of inertia, she may capsize.

Once a boat is on, or beyond, her beam ends she is going to become more interested in her GZ curve, and a heavy rig will work against her. But there is no doubt that when it comes to resisting knockdown, a good solid rig is a help rather than a hindrance. Such a rig also has more chance of staying in the boat undamaged through any traumas which may befall. If you lose your rig altogether your roll moment of inertia almost disappears, and you become vulnerable in the extreme.

CONCLUSIONS

What does all this mean for Boats A, B and C?

Boat A emerges with a reasonable GZ curve, a high value for roll moment of inertia, and plenty of displacement.

Boat B has an excellent GZ curve, a modest displacement, and a roll moment of inertia one could live with.

Boat C's GZ curve is less than a pretty sight. Her displacement may well have been eroded close to or even beyond safe limits in the search for sailing performance and cheap construction, although her roll moment of inertia, if she is a cruising boat with a comparatively heavy rig, may be little worse than Boat B.

> Boat A's resistance to capsize is best, followed by Boat B. Boat C is well behind; she is much the likeliest of the three to suffer a capsize and she is also the most vulnerable when in a capsized state.

FURTHER CONSIDERATIONS

A boat's performance in rough weather may be only one of the factors to consider when deciding what sort of boat you should be sailing. Boats of type A tend to be comparatively slow in light airs, expensive to buy and are relatively less roomy down below. Boats like our Boat C are light, airy, spacious and usually sail excellently on good days. They also handle beautifully under power in the absence of crosswinds.

The world is still waiting, and will wait, for a long time yet, for the boat that is all things to all men.

8

RIDING OUT A GALE AT SEA

When discussing storm survival many people become dogmatic about what should and should not be done. I would suggest that there is no single answer to such a question and that your decisions should be based on an informed appraisal of what seems right for your boat and your crew on the day. The important thing is to be aware of the options so that you can choose the best one for the conditions.

Sooner or later, all boats bound on passages beyond a single day's duration are stuck with a gale at sea. The way you choose to ride it out will depend on three things:

- Your tactical situation: that is, your position relative to your destination and any land masses or other dangers
- Your boat's capabilities
- Your crew strength

TACTICAL CONSIDERATIONS

It is common sense that if the gale is 'going your way' and you are not short of sea room you will run with it for as long as you can. Running also happens to be one of the recognised survival techniques, so you may do yourself a double favour so long as you can carry on in safety.

On the other hand, if a lee shore is too close for comfort you will need to opt for one of the techniques designed to maintain your weather gauge. In some boats it will be sufficient to heave-to, while in others this could be suicidal.

If you are well offshore, and sea room is of no consideration, and if you can no longer safely or comfortably sail your course, you will need to decide either to opt for one of the passive techniques (where the boat looks after herself and her crew), or an active technique (where you look after the boat):

- **Passive techniques** include heaving-to, deploying some sort of sea anchor or drogue and lying a'hull
- **Active techniques** include running off, sailing (or motor-sailing) to windward, and heaving-to under power (or sail-assisted power)

PASSIVE TECHNIQUES

When you have a weak or tired crew, or when conditions are of such severity that no-one wants to go on deck if it can be avoided, it is wonderful to be able to leave a boat to look after herself. Unfortunately, not all boats can do this, as we shall see.

HEAVING-TO

When discussing the question of headsail changes in Chapter 4 we looked at the basic proposition of heaving-to. If a boat heaves-to well this gives her an excellent option in any weather in which she can carry canvas. The sails will steady her, and she will head up to the seas at an average of four or five points off (45-55 degrees).

The easiest way to heave-to is to tack with a small or very much reduced headsail onto a tight headsail sheet, but if you would rather heave-to on your current tack and you don't want to work too hard winding the headsail across to weather, then run off and pull the sail over in the reduced apparent wind, bring the boat to, and lash the helm 'down'. In practical terms, this means lash the tiller to leeward, or steer a wheel hard to windward and put the brake on.

Hove-to

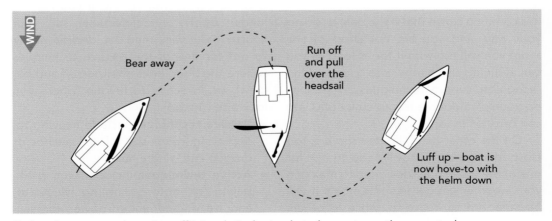

WIND

Bear away

Run off and pull over the headsail

Luff up – boat is now hove-to with the helm down

By bearing away and running off it is relatively simple to heave-to on the same tack

When it is time to let draw and get back under way you can do so by simply unlashing the helm and bringing it across to windward. If the boat is well-balanced, she will bear away and gybe, her mainsheet already being well in and under control. The headsail will then be on the 'right' side and off you will go.

If you want to let draw on the tack on which you are hove-to, you have only to let the headsail pass across to the leeward side and sail away.

You can usually persuade a boat to go roughly where you want when she is hove-to by juggling the sheets. If you pull the jib hard up to windward and ease the main a few feet, she will stop as near dead as it is possible for her to do. Ease the jib progressively and she begins to fore-reach, moving ahead with an ever-decreasing amount of leeway as the clew of the sail comes closer to the midships position.

Some boats will fore-reach to windward with the helm left free and the jib clew pinned amidships by both sheets. Once balanced, such boats will jog slowly to weather, not pointing high, but not soaking anyone to the skin either.

Sort out what you need for your tactical situation, and what is making the boat lie as quietly as possible. When you have arranged the boat as you want her, check your drift. Use your hand-bearing compass to sight along the slick you are leaving.

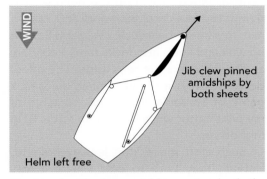

Pinning the jib clew amidships using both the sheets will make some boats fore-reach to windward

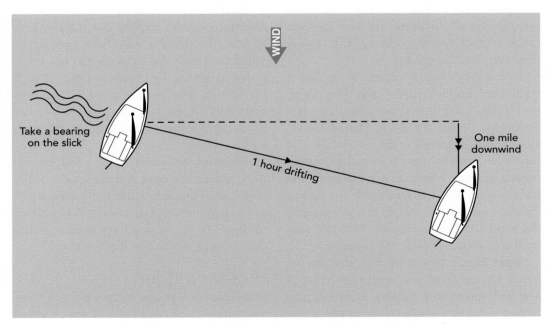

Take a bearing on the slick and work out the reciprocal to find your heading. If you can estimate your drift speed you can plot hourly

The bearing of the slick is the reciprocal of your heading. You can also make a surprisingly good estimate of the speed of your drift. Log the two figures and you'll be able to keep your plot going through the worst of the weather even if Captain GPS goes absent without leave.

Boat A from Chapter 7 heaves-to beautifully. Any time you are sick of going to windward you can tack, leave the headsail where it is, lash the helm so it is trying to steer into the wind and take a rest. In a heavy gale such a vessel will point up well and keep her decks remarkably dry as she shoulders the seas aside. The effect down below is a dream. I once enjoyed a game of Scrabble on the saloon table of my pilot cutter while hove-to in force 10 in mid-ocean.

Such craft make little leeway hove-to; instead, they tend to drift square across the wind. In a force 8 gale a 32-foot heavy displacement boat would make no more than a mile downwind in one hour. A bigger boat makes less than this when hove-to 'dead'. Arrange for her to fore-reach a touch and you can cut the leeway down to next to nothing.

If the boat has a plumb stem like a traditional English cutter, she may lie-to satisfactorily with a staysail only – the clew amidships – and the helm lashed down. Leeway will increase a lot, but if there is too much wind to carry a trysail, a double-reefed staysail alone is a halfway house before lying a'hull. A boat with a cutaway forefoot will not do this as she will lie with the wind abaft the beam and take the seas on the quarter, which is not pleasant.

Boat B will heave-to, but she will lie much further from the wind than Boat A and will make more leeway – anything up to two knots in a whole gale. However, she should be safe enough unless she finds she is being knocked down heavily, because

although she is tending to lie beam-on to the seas, her resistance to capsize is fairly high. But keep a close watch on developments, because if the seas grow steeper she may not be able to cope. Boats of this type fore-reach beautifully with the headsail amidships.

Boat C may well not heave-to at all. Some will, but all are going to be knocked around by the waves and some cannot be trusted not to tack themselves as soon as you have shut the hatch. They also make a great deal of leeway, having almost no lateral resistance with the keel stalled. They generally lie beam-on or worse. Since their knockdown potential is high, heaving-to is not a good idea.

LYING A'HULL & PARA ANCHORS

When a vessel is allowed to drift freely with the wind and sea, showing no canvas and not using her engine, she is said to be lying a'hull.

Sometimes a boat will heave-to under minimum canvas to ride out a gale, only to find later that the wind has increased so much that even the little sail she has left is pressing her too far down for safety. That is the time to change tactics. With a suitable boat and a crew fatigue problem you will probably decide to drag down the sails and lie a'hull.

Whether this is a good idea or not depends on the boat and steepness of the seas, but in the last resort, if the crew is sick or too exhausted to run, and it is too windy to heave-to unless you have a para anchor or a drogue, it's lie a'hull or nothing.

THE PARA ANCHOR
Many modern yachts simply do not have the option to heave to in a storm by virtue of their hull and rig configuration. Most boats of less than 45 feet (14 metres) or so

can be talked into heaving to and pointing as high as her skipper wishes by deploying a para anchor.

The para anchor is like an airman's parachute in the water. It is generally streamed from the bow, but if its warp is led directly from the bow roller, it leaves the boat lying dead head to wind, which may compromise the rudder if the boat falls back on it. In any case, the shoulder-first attitude of the truly hove-to yacht is hard to beat.

The way around this is to lead a spring line via a snatch block from the quarter and rolling-hitch it to the warp at the bow. Now ease the warp and the spring line so

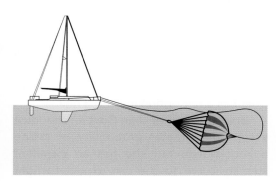

A para anchor

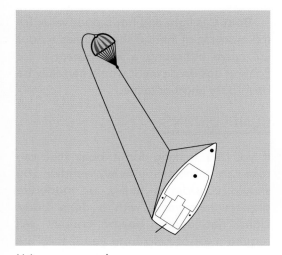

Using a para anchor

that the hitch is a boat's length or more from the stem head. By winching in on the spring, the boat's angle to the action can be adjusted to find the optimum. The skipper might experiment with a little sail to steady the boat, but often she will be better off under bare poles. Only experiment can show what's best for the boat on the day.

The slick left by the para anchor as the yacht drifts to leeward helps calm the worst of the seas and the technique goes a long way towards making up the shortfall in the modern yacht's options. It should go without saying that chafe is an issue never to be ignored.

LYING A'HULL

Given that all your deck stowage arrangements, particularly your sail lashings, are able to resist deliberate sabotage, the only job that remains before battening down and leaving the boat to her own devices is to decide what to do with the helm.

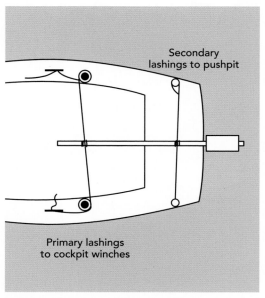

To keep the tiller in one piece when lying a'hull put two lashings on it – one at the end, and one near the rudder stock

Bear in mind that the boat is going to be knocked around and that, from time to time, she will gather way. If you lash the helm down to leeward (as for heaving-to) there is a possibility that she may sail herself almost head to wind up the face of a wave, fall back and damage her rudder as she plunges astern onto it. If the rudder were fixed in line with the keel, it would have a better chance of surviving. On the other hand, if you lash the helm amidships the boat is not going to point up at all, so she will be permanently beam-on to what is on the menu. You see the dilemma.

The day will provide the answer, but whatever you do, lash your helm firmly. If you have a tiller, lash it not only at the end but also near the rudder stock, otherwise when you fall off a big wave the leverage of the

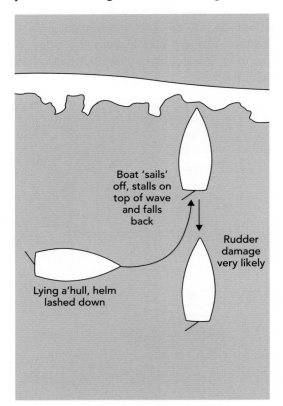

Boat 'sails' off, stalls on top of wave and falls back

Rudder damage very likely

Lying a'hull, helm lashed down

The danger when lying a'hull is that the boat will sail up a wave, fall back and smash her rudder

single lashing at the forward end may allow the force acting on the rudder to break the tiller. I once had this experience and spent the rest of the night half under water with my wife holding onto my boots as I tried to jury-rig a tiller. Not recommended for the faint and weary traveller.

Lying a'hull in a suitable boat is less uncomfortable than you might suppose. One would expect to roll frantically but this is not the case. A solid wind of force 10 or more exerts so much force on the rigging that the boat rarely rolls to windward of the upright position, but because you are lying in the trough of the waves you have to accept the possibility of some sort of a knockdown. For this reason, before deciding to lie a'hull you will need to consider whether it would be a wise move for your boat.

Boat A is heavy, has a beneficial roll moment of inertia and a reasonable GZ curve even if she should be laid over. This boat has a fair option in lying a'hull.

Boat B is lighter than Boat A; she must accept the greater probability of taking a knockdown, but she has an excellent stability curve so she can expect to fight hard and to right herself if she should be unlucky.

Boat C is light and has a poor value for roll moment of inertia; she also has a poor GZ curve indicating a fine potential for floating upside down. It would certainly be best to try another tactic.

CONCLUSIONS

If you are looking for a boat that can take care of herself in heavy weather, you should consider a heavy, or moderate displacement yacht with a deep body. Light, flat-floored, beamy cruisers will require a lot of help from you if they are to come through without embarrassment.

ACTIVE TECHNIQUES

It should by now be clear that there are occasions when positive measures need to be taken if you, your crew and your boat are to survive a blow unscathed. If the boat is constitutionally unable to look after herself all passive techniques must be discounted, but even when a vessel is well suited to passive methods circumstances may dictate a preference for some active effort by her crew. Once again, we'll look at the recognised techniques and place each in the context of how suitable it may be for a particular type of yacht.

RUNNING WITH THE STORM

The most obvious advantage of running off in heavy wind and seas is that the force of both is lessened. If you are trying to sail to windward in an apparent wind of force 10 and you turn and run off at even a sensible speed, your apparent wind drops to a friendly force 8, while the force of any breaking seas is correspondingly less as well.

The second benefit is that you present the boat at a favourable aspect to any seas with the potential to capsize her. Beam-on to the waves she is at her most vulnerable, but if she can take the seas end-on, either bow or stern, she is as safe as she can be.

DANGERS OF RUNNING
POOPING

A vessel is 'pooped' when a breaking wave overwhelms her from the stem. Being pooped is not to be confused with a small crest slopping over the transom and tipping a few gallons of water into the cockpit. If you are ever pooped, you'll know the difference.

A boat can be pooped in any bad sea, but if speed is kept to a sensible level, as described in the section on running in Chapter 4, the risk will be minimised. This is because if you are going too fast, you will be pulling a stern wave which will add itself to any following sea and may persuade it to break with unhappy results.

Because of the danger of pooping, and

Running in heavy weather

also of broaching, it is vital to keep the main companionway battened down when running in heavy weather. If the helmsman feels lonely, tell him to sing a song, but don't leave that top washboard out. You may live to regret it.

BROACHING

The dangers of broaching have been discussed in Chapter 4. They can be minimised by doing all you can to reduce rolling and by sailing at a sensible speed. The use of warps may also help, as we shall see.

Boat about to broach

PITCHPOLING

Pitchpoling is what happens when a boat is running in an exceptionally high, steep sea and she is flipped stern over bow. It is an unlikely contingency outside the Southern Ocean or the North Atlantic 'out of season'. I have no experience of such a situation, but for readers who wish to know more, Bernard Moitessier gives an excellent account in his book *The Long Way*, as does Miles Smeeton in *Once Is Enough*.

SPECIAL TECHNIQUES FOR HEAVY WEATHER RUNNING

The object of the exercise, remember, is to maintain a comfortable speed (see Chapter 4) and to keep steering so as to take the seas more or less 'stern on'.

BARE POLES

As the wind rises and speed gets out of hand, the first thing to do is to remove the last rag of sail and continue under 'bare poles'. This works well in a heavy blow. There is no problem keeping up speed. A heavy displacement 36-footer in severe gale or storm conditions may well find herself 'sailing' at six knots without any difficulty. Try it on a windy day in calm water. See how far off a dead run you have to come before you lose control.

USE OF WARPS

If your speed builds up too much even under bare poles the only way to slow down is to trail something in your wake. The favourite item is a long warp towed in a bight with one end secured to each quarter of the boat. It is best to lead the warp from somewhere forward of the rudder post so that you retain some vestige of steering. If it's led to the winches to secure, you can use them to recover it.

To be of any use at all, a warp must be towed with its bight at least one wave astern of you. If you think you might end up opting for this technique, you need a heavy rope more than 120 metres long. Try trailing the dock lines the manufacturers issue with new boats and you will merely succeed in stripping off the whippings and rendering them even more useless than they already are. Every cruising boat should have one long warp for the day in harbour when nothing else will do. Here is an extra use for it. In the absence of such a line, there is always the kedge warp.

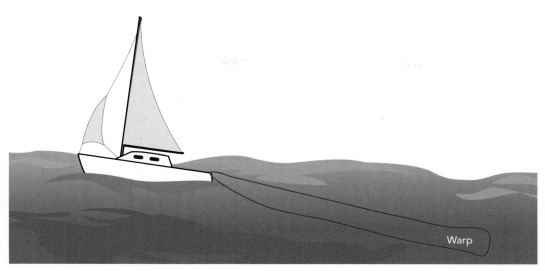

Towing warps

THE DROGUE

In recent years considerable work has been done by various authoritative bodies to test the usefulness of a drogue towed astern while running in heavily breaking seas. A drogue is a recoverable device which floats just below the surface of the water and exerts a strong pull on the rope by which it is streamed from its parent vessel. In cases where the boat needs to be slowed down and her bight of streamed warp is proving inadequate for the purpose, she can deploy her drogue and achieve a far more effective result.

One school of thought even suggests that a vessel can best ride out a storm by simply lying stern-to to such a device and securing the hatches. Her crew are recommended to sit tight down below, restrained by 'aircraft-type safety harnesses'. Perhaps these folk are right but I, for one, can't help wondering what Joshua Slocum would have made of such a theory. The idea of the Old Man happily riding out a gale strapped firmly in his bunk, out of reach of his tobacco, is hard to grasp.

Probably a more useful way to employ a drogue is that practised by many professional powerboat operators such as the RNLI (Royal National Lifeboat Institution). These men and women have found that if they stream a drogue over the stern and then motor ahead against its pull, they achieve excellent downwind (and down-wave) control. This highly effective method could also be considered by a sailing vessel. Instead of running under bare poles she could set a storm jib to provide power and help the rudder to bite, and use the drogue to keep the speed down.

A modern drogue is not a bulky item when stowed, and owners of the type of yacht more prone to rapid drifting in high winds would be well advised to consider including one in their stores list. It is as well to remember, however, that the loads a drogue impose upon a hull are massive (up to 7,500lb for a three-foot diameter drogue!) so its proposed attachment bollard needs to be beyond suspicion of weakness. A further consideration is that during a single average storm the streaming line of a drogue is likely to ease and then take the strain 10,000 times, and it will chafe through long before the storm is over unless the most stringent preventative measures are taken.

If a full-on lifeboat drogue seems too violent an answer, a more yacht-friendly solution seems to be the series drogue.

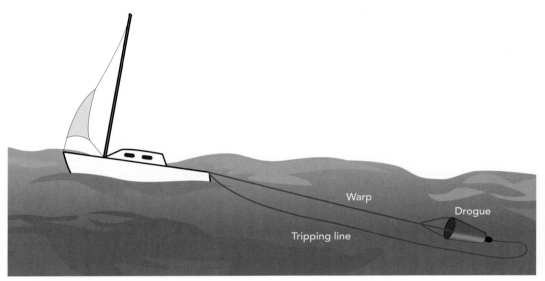

Warp

Drogue

Tripping line

The drogue

THE SERIES DROGUE

This is a development of the single drogue that is finding favour among multihulls and has been used successfully by many monohulls. It is made up of a large number of 5-inch cones 20 inches or so apart on a long nylon line. 100 cones on 16mm line seems to work well for a 5 or 6-ton boat. The outboard extremity carries a weight – often a bight of chain, but conventional anchors have also been used. The long length means that at least some of the cones are always loaded up as waves rise and fall, so the pull is surprisingly steady.

I have no personal experience of using a series drogue, but my old friend Chris Cooling has been working with them. I rely on his sound judgment and experience for the following (and the basis of the diagram):

The whole drogue is streamed from a bridle secured to the quarters with 75-100ft of line between the bridle and the first cone. So long as it has been carefully stowed and isn't in a tangle, a series drogue is simple to set. The best way to do this avoiding big snatch loads when the drogue takes up is to first deploy the bridle, then flake out the drogue bit by bit under the bridle with the extreme end attached to the chain going in last. Theoretically it can be retrieved without a winch or a trip line, but a number of users suggest a floating trip line either of tape or polypropylene rope attached to the extreme end of the chain. Retrieval can otherwise be a time-consuming and energetic business.

Don't forget, if a drogue seems to be slowing you too much for comfort but you need it to maintain an end-on attitude, you can always set a storm jib as well. The strains go up, but it may well be worth trying.

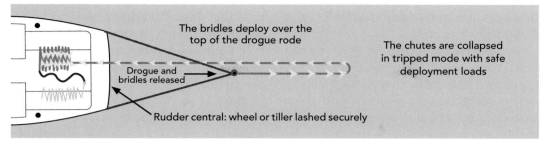

Deploying a series drogue

Use of a trip line is controversial. The chain / weight can be dropped in at this stage without the trip, completing a Conventional Deployment

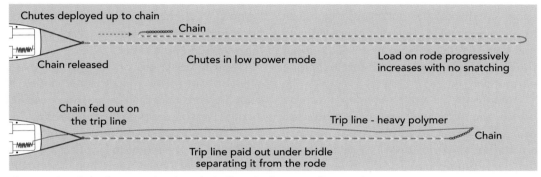

Conventional deployment (top) and trip line deployment (bottom)

CONCLUSIONS ON RUNNING

Boat A runs well. She is not in a hurry to go too fast and with her excellent tracking characteristics she steers like a dream. If she rolls, her helm balance will not be much altered.

Boat B, being lighter than Boat A, is more easily driven and will need extra care to check her speed. She will also demand more of her helmsman, but she is free of any particular vices.

Boat C will have to work hard to keep her speed down. So long as she remains level, she is easy to steer with her big spade rudder. But if she develops a roll or takes on a large angle of heel, she is by far the most likely of the three to overpower her helmsman and broach. This is because her flat floor and beamy shape create a highly asymmetrical hull shape at extreme heel which destroys her helm balance.

SAILING TO WINDWARD & MOTORSAILING

Traditionally this would never have been considered a serious proposition as a survival technique. Modern developments in boat design, however, have made it not only possible but in some cases desirable.

For the boat which is debarred by her shape and concept from being able to look after herself, sailing to windward must be looked at as a way of riding out a moderate gale. The benefits are that the boat will never be beam-on to a steep breaker and because the bow can be presented to a nasty sea at a good speed, the helmsman can go some way towards dodging the really wicked ones. Helming technique of a high calibre is essential and considerable powers of endurance are required, both from the helmsman and those around below as the yacht tries to shake herself to pieces.

A boat is required to be quick on the helm to succeed. She must luff to the crest, then bear away as it passes beneath her so as to avoid the bone- and boat-shattering impact of heavy pounding. Skill and experience will also be needed at the helm to decide how much wind to feed her, whether to sail her 'shy' or 'full and by' and when to do one or the other.

Clearly only a powerful yacht with superbly cut sails and bullet-proof gear can hope to execute such performance. Should you have a roller-reefing headsail 'without the option' you can discount this technique altogether.

However, if your headsails aren't up to the job, you still can motor-sail to windward. Take in your headsail altogether and motor-sail with a board-flat deep-reefed main or the trysail. For a

boat that doesn't perform over well under sail alone, this is a perfectly legitimate technique and has helped many on short-haul voyages where fuel is not an issue. See below for more on the subject.

Boat A is not going to be seriously interested in sailing to windward to survive a gale in open water. She doesn't need to because she can heave-to, saving herself and her crew from a dangerously violent experience. If she were ever in the position of having to do this, she would suffer from being slow on the helm. On the other hand, her comparatively heavy displacement makes pounding a rarity.

Type B boats are on record as having survived storms by using this technique. If such a boat is taking a bad pasting hove-to it could well be the best thing for her to do, if she doesn't care to go a-running.

Boat C can also make good use of this technique. We have seen that she really

Helming to windward

Going to windward in a blow is a test of the helmsman, crew and boat

needs to keep her head up. Here is a possible way for her to do so.

It cannot be overstressed that sailing upwind in a gale is brutally hard on boat and crew. It also requires little imagination to see that sooner or later there may be too much wind to carry on.

HEAVING-TO UNDER SAIL-ASSISTED POWER

One of the favourite survival tricks in a displacement motor yacht or, indeed, a medium-sized fishing boat, is to heave-to under power, using a method known as 'dodging'. The boat is headed into the weather and her throttles are set so as to maintain steerage way, or a touch more.

Nowadays most sailing yachts have powerful auxiliary engines. Maybe not powerful enough to heave-to under engine alone, but if the mainsail or trysail is left setting, sheeted hard amidships, and the engine used to maintain the boat at 20 or 30 degrees from what is coming, the boat is at the best angle to the weather. She can dodge the worst of the seas and you have another survival system which, when all else fails, may be a saviour.

Any of our three types of boat might care to make use of this, but how effective it is will depend on the engine and the type and siting of the propeller. For Boat C particularly if she is small and has a poor suit of sails, the method may prove to be of great importance.

GENERAL REMARKS

No matter what shape a boat is, there is no argument about the fact that, all other things being equal, the bigger she is the safer she will be. Nonetheless tiny vessels have made some remarkable voyages on the ping-pong ball principle – that so long as watertight integrity is unbreached, and no bones or spars are broken, all will be well. This is a point of view.

It should be a natural priority to pay attention to ensuring that everything on board will stay in its place in the event of a knockdown. No-one of sound mind would quarrel with this, but how much happier would we be if our boats were of a type unlikely to be knocked down in the first place.

Each owner must ask himself what his true requirements are when he or she is selecting a boat, and the answers must be honest.

A well-found yacht of sensible design and construction should be able to enjoy year after year of cruising without drama.

A skipper and crew who continue to temper boldness with a sound, seamanlike approach will give her all the chance she needs to prove herself fit for the sea. Between them they will be able to take in their stride whatever the weather brings. Indeed, it will be their pride to do so.

It is the ability, bred by necessity, to solve their own problems that has set sailors apart down the ages. Self-sufficiency has always been their cornerstone, and today's yachtsmen must carry that legacy with an increasing sense of responsibility because, as communications improve, it is becoming easier every year to cry for outside assistance as soon as something goes amiss.

While the sea can provide almost endless recreation and sheer pleasure, it can occasionally turn into a hostile environment whose sphere humanity enters at their peril. We should treat it with the respect that is, and always will be, its proper due.

9

SHELTER FROM THE STORM

ANCHORING

When all else has failed and your boat is driving down onto a lee shore despite your best efforts with the sails and engine, you still have your ground tackle. Anchoring off the beach has been known to save vessels that could otherwise have been lost. There is no special secret for this; the same principles apply as in any other circumstances:

- Use the biggest and best anchor you can carry
- Use the longest possible scope of cable – the heavier the better

We all have our own favourite type of anchor. At the time of writing, I favour an old-fashioned Bruce which has never let me down in the eleven seasons we've shared, but it's every man to this own here. Just buy a really good one and make it the biggest your boat can sensibly carry. Don't expect the toy that arrives as part of a production boat package to be good for more than a lunch hook.

Cable is a more complicated subject.

Chain cable has much in its favour. By virtue of its weight, it assists the holding power of an anchor. For the same reason it requires a shorter scope than rope, or to put it another way, a given scope will do more good. Chain doesn't chafe, either on the stem head or the seabed, so it won't part in the night. It is easy to clean, and it self-stows if you have a decent cable locker.

On the other hand, it is noisy, expensive and if it is heavy enough to do any good, it will require the services of a windlass in any boat much over 32 feet long. A windlass will probably be electric with the works protected by what is called a 'slow-blow' fuse. This can readily be reset by hand, but a skipper must know where it is and have practised resetting it, since if it blows in action, time may be limited to say the least.

A manual windlass must be a meaty piece of equipment with a proper handle sited so that a person can throw his weight at it. Vertical-shaft hand-cranked windlasses are not a lot of use generally. A horizontal shaft and a good warping drum as well as the chain gypsy can be a blessing.

The hidden problem of chain cable is that in exceptionally violent conditions, no matter what the scope, it can still snub up bar tight. If this happens you are in danger of plucking out your anchor, and this is where nylon warp comes in.

Nylon warp is super-springy. Its elasticity gives it tremendous strength and a boat riding to it will never snatch at her anchor. It is cheaper than chain and can be used on larger boats without a windlass, but it is subject to chafe. Furthermore, to give an anchor with warp the holding power it would have with chain you will need twice as much scope.

The best solution for heavy weather anchoring, particularly on a lee shore in a bad sea, is to ease out a long scope of chain and then attach a hefty length of nylon warp into the bight of the chain using a chain hook before it has all run out. Now lie to the warp but make sure the chain is all fast inboard to take up the task in case of chafe on the rode. This gives the best of both worlds. If your anchor won't hold now, you can do no more.

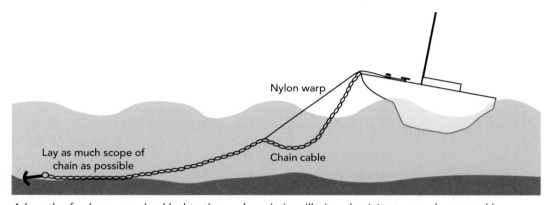

A length of nylon warp shackled to the anchor chain will give elasticity to your heavy tackle

SELECTING A BERTH

Once you have arrived at your chosen anchorage you have to decide where to lie. You'll be looking for a spot as close as possible to a weather shore, keeping the fetch of wavelets down to a minimum but taking account of any predicted windshifts. You don't want to swing up the beach in the night and since you are going to lay a monumental scope of cable, swinging room is something to be taken seriously.

Given that you have plenty of good tackle and your boat behaves herself at anchor, your greatest danger is that of other boats dragging down on you. Foresee it and select a berth that will minimise this possibility.

LYING TO TWO ANCHORS

If you are lying in a sheltered roadstead with no particular tide affecting you, it will do no harm to lay a second anchor if you are in doubt about whether your bower (main anchor) will hold.

The best way to arrange the anchors is a Y-shape from the bows. If your bower is on chain and your kedge is on warp and chain (even if the cable is all rope, there should be at least four metres of chain between the end of the warp and the anchor) you can pull in on the kedge warp until you see the bower cable sag a little. This shows that the weight is being shared. The anchors are then balanced, with each taking some of the load.

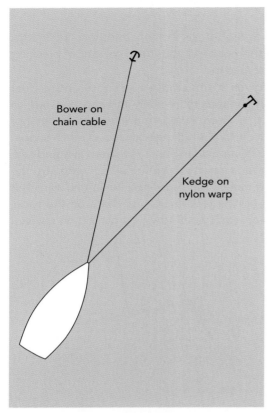

Bower on
chain cable

Kedge on
nylon warp

If you need to lie to two anchors lay them in Y-formation, adjusting them as you swing

LAYING A SECOND ANCHOR

When your bower is on chain it's awkward to say the least to use the yacht to lay out a second anchor. If you have a decent dinghy, the best way to lay your kedge is simply to row it out. Lower the anchor into the small boat over the bow. Now follow it up with all the chain and warp you plan to lay. If the anchor goes into the boat first, the cable will flake itself naturally as you lower it down, making sure it runs clean. Next, make the end of the warp fast on board, hop into the dinghy and off you go, paying out cable until it's all gone. Then drop the hook, making sure your foot is not trapped when you heave it over the stern. Now scramble back on board and heave away until the anchor takes a bite.

If your main hook is on warp you can generally motor up to where you want to place your kedge, gathering slack on the bower rode as you go. Now drop the kedge and fall back, evening up the warps. If you have a handy boat and the bower anchor is on warp, it is quite possible to sail up to the spot for letting go the kedge, but it's a lot easier to use the motor if you have one.

SWINGING WITH TWO ANCHORS DOWN

If you should swing more than a few degrees when you are lying to two anchors, you will need to adjust the cables to even up the pull. If you swing so far that they come into line they may well interfere with one another so that you have to recover one and re-lay it. A thorough nuisance. If the situation with the wind is unstable, therefore, it is much less trouble to lie to one reliable anchor and lots of scope.

WEIGHTING THE CABLE

An excellent way of augmenting the holding power of an anchor without increasing the scope of the cable is to lower a weight down the cable so that it is suspended halfway to the seabed. This has the effect of depressing the catenary angle of the cable, thus pulling on the anchor at a more efficient angle. It also resists the tendency to snub. Patent weights designed for this purpose are available. but you can always make one up by shackling a spare anchor, a pig of ballast, or a suitably loaded mutineer into the bight of the cable and lowering away.

For more on anchor weights, see my YouTube video on my channel.

Scan to watch this video

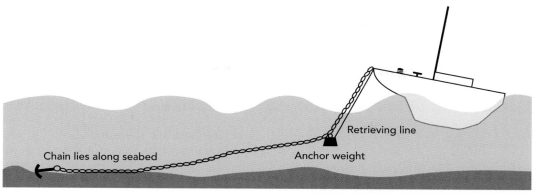

A big anchor weight lowered down the cable on a big shackle holds the chain at an efficient angle to the seabed and reduces the risk of snubbing. It will also stop the boat surging around and let you sleep

WINDAGE

The windage of your boat's hull, mast and superstructure is something over which you have no control, but there is plenty of additional windage that you can do something to reduce. If it looks like being touch and go for your anchor, every little helps.

Here are some of the items which are easily removed, and which could make all the difference:

- Dodgers and sprayhoods can add up to a sail area equivalent to a sizeable trysail
- Flags, burgees and washing
- Stowed sails, particularly furled roller headsails
- Radar reflectors
- External halyards – take them down and leave a light 'sleeper' up there, but only if your engine is bullet-proof and you have no plans to leave any time soon. A 16mm halyard going up and down a 45ft mast generates almost 5 square feet of windage. Try holding a 5 x 1 sheet of plywood up across a 40-knot wind …
- Any other deck hamper
- And finally, don't forget that the sail area of three big guys standing around on the foredeck is substantial

MOORINGS

If there are vacant mooring buoys in your harbour of refuge it is always tempting to use one instead of anchoring. If you are considering doing this, one or two rules apply:

- Never lie to a mooring unless you have good reason to believe that it is in first class condition, and of a suitable size for your boat.
- Never lie for more than a few minutes to a slip rope as these are prone to chafe. In rough weather it's best to shackle your

anchor chain to the mooring if you can stand the noise, because doing so will remove any danger resulting from chafe. This is rather a cumbersome procedure, however, and if there is a chance of wanting to leave in a hurry it may be best to avoid it.

- It is a sound idea to lie to a round turn and a bowline. The round turn will absorb the chafe and if you make the bowline loop good and long you will be able to untie it without going into an attitude of prayer over the bow.

- If you are going to make fast with a line or with your chain, leave a slip rope loose on the buoy as a back-up. With the slack taken out, a slip rope also serves to relieve the main mooring line while you are securing or removing it.

LYING ALONGSIDE

RAFT-UPS

Raft-ups are always a mixed blessing. In a gale, avoid lee-shore raft-ups as you would the plague. On a sheltered shore with the wind blowing straight off it, so long as the boats are arranged in a sensible order of size and are properly secured with shore lines, breast ropes and springs, you may get some sleep if the water remains calm and no one wants to leave. Should the situation be deficient in any of these requirements bad tempers and broken boats are the

Raft-ups are OK when it's calm, but avoid them in stormy conditions

inevitable result. If the water chops up, you can guarantee that someone's fenders will jump up over the rail and then there will be trouble.

Probably the most dangerous contingency is that of two boats rolling together and damaging one another's spreaders. This can be avoided by making sure that no two masts are adjacent.

To lie on the inside of a raft in a berth that is rapidly becoming untenable while those outside you vacillate is a wretched position to be in. The way to be sure of never experiencing it is to have nothing to do with raft-ups on windy days. It may be tempting to go for the imaginary security of the dock wall and the crowd, but you could well be much safer, and you will certainly be a lot quieter, if you anchor away from the mob.

THE WEATHER BERTH

Even if nobody has rafted up to you, when you are being blown hard against a wall to which you have tied yourself you must make sure you are not pinned onto it by the rising wind and sea. You must also avoid damage while struggling to get off.

When you need to leave an ugly weather berth there are a number of ways to help the boat off the wall. The first thing to try is bearing off with a spar. You'll probably use a boathook or spinnaker pole. If it's blowing hard this may not work, so the next attempt will be to spring off by either the head or the stern. Do both while bearing off if it helps.

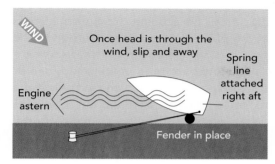

Springing off by the stern

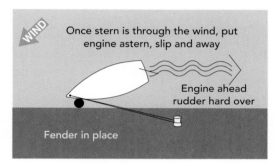

Springing off by the head
By careful manipulation of warps, fenders and engine power it may be possible to spring the boat off a weather berth

This should do the trick. Note that unless you have a bow thruster to assist, you may find it's better to spring the stern out and go off astern. Springing will be more efficient with the propeller wash driving directly onto the turned rudder, and most sailing boats have a natural tendency to lie with the stern upwind when in 'free float'. As you leave astern, you aren't fighting the yacht's nature, as you are when going out bow first.

If springing fails, you'll need to pull yourself off. If there is a handy post, mooring buoy or some other fixed object up to windward row a line across, rig it back to the foredeck and pull – or winch – the ship's head up to the wind. If you've no foredeck windlass, you can rig a snatch block near the bow and lead the line to a sheet winch.

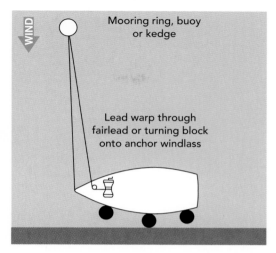

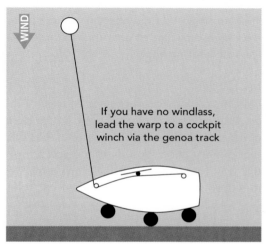

If there is a suitable post or mooring ring to windward you may be able to warp the boat off the wall using the anchor windlass or a sheet winch

If there is nothing to secure a line to you will have to kedge off. Row your kedge well out to windward and then proceed as above.

When circumstances are such that your boat is pounding in a weather berth and there is no available alternative, you can ease the pain by rowing out your kedge amidships and using it to hold yourself off the wall with a bridle rigged fore and aft to keep the yacht parallel.

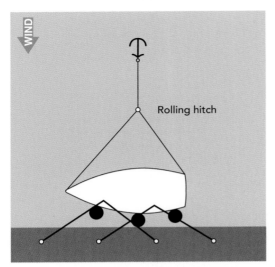

If all else fails, hold the boat off the wall using the kedge, attaching the stern line to the kedge line with a rolling hitch

FENDERS

Fenders are obviously the secret to survival on a hostile wall. Like anchors, fenders need to be big. Take the manufacturer's recommendation, double it and you are on the way to success, but far more effective in extremis is the humble honest car tyre.

These can be acquired from most dumps at the popular price and conversion to the world's most effective boat-saver consists of gouging two holes in the tread, one at the top for the rope and one at the bottom to let the dirty water drain out. Car tyres aren't pretty and some damage to the topside finish is almost inevitable, but when all seems lost they are a whole lot better than a smashed-in toe rail and a gel coat scuffed through to the mat inside.

Beware of tying up to a lee shore, and if you do, use big fenders unlike here

CLEARING OUT

Any roadstead or harbour with one side open to the sea has the capacity to change at the caprice of the weather from a sheltered haven into a deadly trap.

As soon as the wind begins to blast straight into your anchorage it's time to go. Never mind what the others are doing. When in doubt, clear out; particularly if night is coming on and you know you would be safer at sea. It doesn't happen often, but when it does, you'll know what you have to do.

With luck there will be another bay around the corner, open to the previous wind direction but now sheltered, to which you can shift your berth. If there isn't, you will just have to grab as much sea room as you can and then ride it out. Many a boat has been saved by doing so.

When the bay is unlit, night is falling and you are having doubts, take a bearing on a safe path to the entrance. Should the worst happen and you have to clear out, you've only to weigh anchor, steer the course and you're out, free and safe even if you can't see a thing.

10
EMERGENCIES

Emergencies involving people or gear can happen at any time. Fire, in particular, is just as likely to break out in good weather as in bad. For most common crises, however, heavy conditions can act as a catalyst. The sort of shaking and pounding a yacht takes in a steep sea will seek out any weaknesses in her gear. Split pins not properly opened may work their way loose, excess loads can bring a stranding steering wire to a sudden end, untidy ropes that have been left habitually lying on a side deck are readily washed overboard into the propeller, and the mortal danger of losing a crew member over the side is many times multiplied. In this chapter we'll consider how to handle some of the main emergencies which heavy weather may exacerbate.

RIG FAILURE

STANDING RIGGING

The stainless-steel wire standing rigging favoured by most modern cruising yachts is strong and stable, and the fittings by which it is attached to masts and rigging screws are extremely reliable when one considers the snatching loads to which rough seas can subject them. As previously noted, however, despite the excellence of today's gear, rigging failure has not been entirely eliminated from the modern cruiser's life.

If it is to let go, rigging almost invariably fractures where the wire joins the terminal fitting, especially where there is no proper arrangement for 'universal movement'. The working life of a rig is not indefinite, so keep an eye on it on a regular basis, both aloft and at deck level. If it's ten years old and has done some miles, it's probably time to replace it.

The first sign of failure in a 1 x 19 stainless-steel wire will probably be the parting of a single strand. As soon as this is spotted something must be done, because not only has a proportion of the strength of the wire been lost; where one strand has parted more are liable to follow.

SHROUD FAILURE

Rigging failure can mean instant dismasting, but you may be able to save yourself if you are able to tack immediately you see a shroud on the windward side fail or begin to strand. Better still, slam the helm down, leave the jibsheet cleated, and heave-to on the opposite tack. Both actions relieve the damaged wire, allowing you time to think, but every second counts. There is no time to waste admiring the banana-shaped mast.

FORESTAY OR BACKSTAY FAILURE

A mast may be in dire straits following the loss of a shroud, but when a forestay or a backstay carries away, it will be lucky to survive. In the case of a boat with fore-and-aft sets of lower shrouds, however, there is always a slim chance that if the backstay lets go, the lowers and the leech of a close-hauled mainsail, coupled with the mainsheet, will hold it up long enough for you to take action. In the same way, a broken forestay may be sufficiently backed up by the jib luff or a halyard stowed on the pulpit combined with a babystay.

These natural expedients may hold things together for a few seconds while you manoeuvre, but if you blink one too many times you may lose the lot. It should go without saying that if a forestay breaks, you must immediately run off the wind, removing all the strain. Luffing will possibly save the mast if the backstay parts.

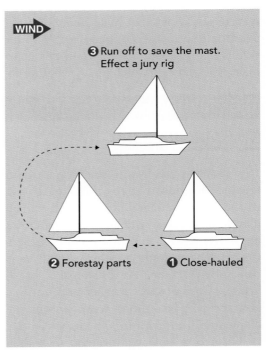

If the forestay fails, bear away onto a run immediately

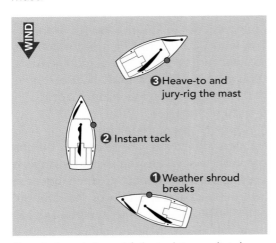

If a windward shroud fails, tack immediately

GETTING TO HARBOUR

If a shroud has failed it can sometimes pay to keep your sails up. At least they are steadying the boat and reducing that tendency to roll sharply, which is the worst thing that can happen. As soon as you have manoeuvred to place the damage onto the lee side, you should take steps to set up the most convenient item of spare running rigging in place of the lost wire. The main halyard, for example, may well prove the most effective jury backstay, especially if it is of low-stretch super-strong Dyneema.

Where a cap shroud has parted, if it is too dangerous to send a climber up to the spreaders to lead a halyard to the deck, extra 'spread' can sometimes be arranged by passing a jury shroud, usually the spinnaker halyard, through the beak of a well-guyed spinnaker pole before winching it tight.

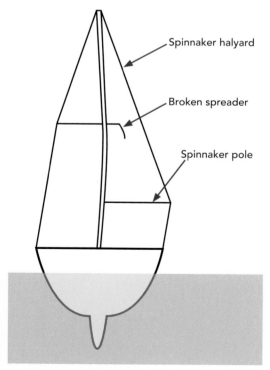

Spinnaker halyard

Broken spreader

Spinnaker pole

Broken spreader jury rig

LONGER-TERM REPAIRS

DYNEEMA BACKUP

All yachts venturing far offshore must stow as part of their essential spares a coil of rigging grade Dyneema a good bit longer than the longest stay. Being basically rope, this is easier to work with than wire and if a Brummel splice has already been made in one end you are halfway there.

Consider how this is to be secured to the rigging screw that will tension it or, if this proves impossible, what alterative means are to be employed to supply the tension. It may not be possible to deploy this at the height of the gale, but when things have quietened down you will probably be able to affect a complete repair with little trouble and so continue your cruise without further disruption.

Dyneema is now specified for standing rigging on some cruising yachts, so there are no worries about it being strong enough for the job. Yachts have crossed oceans like this. The secret is a decent spares kit made up with careful forethought, and don't forget to pack a set of splicing fids and an instruction sheet for making a Brummel splice. Believe me, it's dead easy but you will need a blow-by-blow account of how to do it.

DISMASTING

It is unusual for crew personnel to be injured during the process of dismasting. However, the yacht herself is under serious threat immediately afterwards from the lengths of aluminium tubing backed up by rope, wire and sailcloth slamming into her thin hull. Spars floating alongside in a seaway can do terrible damage. They can even sink the boat.

If the mast goes by the board, first check that the crew are safe, and arrange assistance for any that are not. Then take stock.

There is a natural tendency for people to run around and act on their immediate impressions in an emergency such as this, but it is interesting to note that when that most experienced of seamen, Robin Knox-Johnston, lost both masts from his ketch *Suhaili* in mid-Atlantic, his immediate action after clearing away any wreckage that placed him in obvious danger was to send the troops below for a rest and a good breakfast. With this tucked away, they took a fresh point of view and successfully fetched the Azores under jury rig.

Whatever your circumstances, the vital thing not to do straight after a dismasting is to start the engine. A disabled propeller is virtually guaranteed from all that rubbish in the water, and this will deprive you of your most obvious means of arriving at a safe haven without troubling the Search and Rescue services.

A boat robbed of the roll inertia of her mast leaps around like a lunatic in a rough sea. Her motion will be far more violent than her crew expect, so advise deck workers to clip on to the jackstays, particularly if the guardrails have been carried away.

The first question is whether or not to jettison the mast.

In mid-ocean, you might be well advised to save what you can, because the remains may represent your best chance of building a jury rig.

Within engine range of harbour, the question is rather different. The pile of junk in the water may prove to be good for very little and is probably insured anyway. Your underwriters might initially be less than delighted if you commit it to the deep, but they may change their opinion after they have taken time to consider. After all, if you had saved the insured property only to see it knock a hole through the boat and sink her, their whole risk would go to Davy Jones.

When you have dealt with the mast, make absolutely certain that there are no stray ropes or wires under the water, then start the engine. If the mast has been saved and is towing alongside, continuing 100% vigilance will be needed to ensure that no spare ropes go anywhere near the propeller. More than one simple dismasting has been transformed into disaster by the propeller grabbing the one halyard that was left trailing.

If you're dismasted, tidy everything up

ENGINE FAILURE

It is not at all unusual for a diesel engine which has worked perfectly all season in calm or moderate conditions to falter and die when the boat is rattled about like a cocktail shaker. The reason is almost certainly blocked fuel filters, with air in the injector pump as the direct result. It doesn't take a bucketful of sludge to foul a single paper filter element, and if your tanks have not been cleaned out for a number of years, or even if you have been unfortunate enough to score a fill of dirty diesel, the filter will clog and the engine will slow down, then stop.

The only remedy, as noted in Chapter 2, is to fit a new filter and bleed the fuel system. Most small yacht systems have two diesel filters. One in the fuel line and one on the engine itself. The likely culprit is the first one – the big one in the fuel line.

That's the first to intercept the rubbish, so that's almost certainly where it will be. Get it changed then bleed the system through to purge it of any air. All will then very likely be well.

If affairs in the tank are really desperate you may have to repeat the ghastly operation and you may even have to attend to the engine filter, but this is rare in a small modern yacht.

The most important item, in addition to having at least two spare primary filter elements in stock, is that you know the procedure for your own boat before you have to execute it on a dark night in 10ft-high square waves.

If you haven't actually had to bleed your filter body and injector pump yet, find out where the bleed screws are, and make sure you have a spanner that fits.

BLEEDING THE FUEL SYSTEM

After changing the filter element, the fuel system must be bled to remove any air. First identify, then open the bleed screw on the filter housing. A small hand priming lever will be found on the lift pump usually near the bottom of the engine. In any case it can be located by following the fuel line. Pump this until clear fuel without bubbles flows out of the bleed screw. Keep pumping as the bleed screw is tightened down. This is normally the high point in the low-pressure system. If it is not, then it may be necessary to bleed air from another point, perhaps the engine-mounted filter or even the high-pressure injector pump.

If the engine does need bleeding from the high-pressure injector pump, refer to the manufacturer's instructions. It is easy to undo the wrong screw on the pump and upset the settings.

Many modern engines incorporate self-bleeding devices which can cope with minor leakages once the in-line filter has been purged of air.

Bleed screw

Priming lever

Bleeding screw and priming lever

REPLACING THE FUEL FILTER

Modern fine fuel filters like this are disposable. To change, simply unscrew the old filter using a strap spanner if necessary. Fit the new one, which needs to be tightened only to hand pressure. A smear of fuel on the sealing ring will help it seat properly. The fuel line will need to be bled to remove air from the system.

Primary filter (unfortunately with diesel bug inside it)

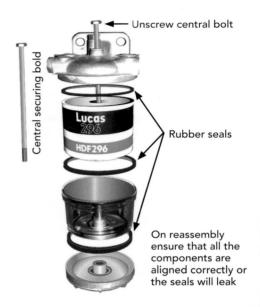

Unscrew central bolt

Central securing bold

Rubber seals

On reassembly ensure that all the components are aligned correctly or the seals will leak

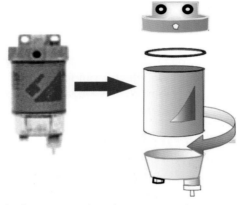

The basic procedure for servicing the primary filter

Lucas and CAV-type filters with a single central bolt need particular care when you reassemble them: unless they are assembled absolutely square, they will leak when you refill them with fuel

ROPES IN THE PROPELLER

Ropes around the propeller are an ever-present danger for any power-driven craft with less line-mangling capacity than a fishing trawler. You can be unlucky any time on passage and pick up a free-floating length of hawser. You might run over a lobster pot in the dark, or somebody else's anchor warp while manoeuvring into a stern-to berth, but none of these are weather-related.

In a hard blow, however, your chances of wrapping up the propeller. with one of your own lines are much increased. Halyards wash off cleats and sheet tails find their way over the quarters, particularly in the dark. If you are relying on your engine as a survival option, to lose it like this would be a nonsense.

At the worst end of the scale, one unhappy sailor is on record as having wrapped the main halyard around the propeller in a rapidly rising wind. It was an internal halyard and the only answer he found was to cut it, losing both engine and mainsail.

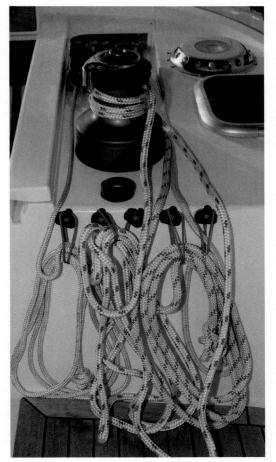

Make sure all ropes are secured and cannot go overboard

then double-check before you put the power into gear.

If all your precautions fail and you do foul the propeller, you are in bad shape, but all may not be lost. There is still a small chance that you can clear it from on board. If the engine is running when a rope is drawn into the vortex, you must act instantly and automatically.

Throw the gears into neutral, just as you should whenever there is the slightest suspicion that a rope could have been dropped over the side, or that you are passing a submerged line. If the propeller turns out to be fouled, try to get a hold on the rope. If it is a sheet or halyard, one end will be made fast aboard, so you should be able to manage this easily.

The rope went on with the propeller driving ahead. If you can reverse that direction of revolution while pulling steadily on the line, there is a chance you may be able to wind it back off again. This is best achieved by decompressing the engine if this is possible, putting the gearbox into astern, then turning the engine slowly over with the stop button 'on' to make sure it doesn't fire up, using the starter motor or, better still, the cranking handle, while one of your crew pulls on the offending line.

If this doesn't work, you are a pure sailing boat until you can regain calm-enough water to dive and unwrap the knitting, or can dry out on the tide and untangle things at your leisure.

The only solution to this dismal problem is to make absolutely sure that no rope can possibly escape over the side, ever. It is good practice always to check around the boat by eye before starting up the engine,

STEERING FAILURE

WHEEL STEERING

The first action when a wheel steering mechanism fails is to deploy the emergency tiller. If the builders have not supplied one, the skipper should set this to rights when preparing the yacht for sea.

Some emergency tillers are so easy to fit and operate that the boat can be sailed comfortably to a safe haven using them.

Others are too short, work backwards, or have to be operated by a gorilla locked under the double bunk in the aft cabin. In such cases it is preferable to try to fix the primary steering system once the emergency tiller is fitted. Apart from the universally awkward nature of access to such systems, the main problem will be to keep the rudder still. Without the emergency tiller this may prove dangerous, impossible, or both. With the tiller attached, the yacht can heave to, keeping the rudder at a constant angle which may be adjusted to help engage the wires onto turning blocks or quadrants.

An emergency tiller attached to a Hydrovane autopilot

AUTOPILOT SALVATION

It's a happy chance that many a modern below-decks autopilot works by means of a ram connected directly to the steering quadrant on the rudder stock. It is thus independent of the wheel steering arrangements and can steer a yacht with disabled steering to safety with no fuss at all. It may help to proceed under short canvas to aid it in its efforts. But it really does work.

RUDDER LOSS

Every sailor must have a complete understanding of rig and hull balance and the way these variable components affect the yacht's steering. When the rudder is lost these factors become vital, because no lashed-up jury rudder works nearly as well as the original, so any help you can give it by controlling heel and sail trim will be crucial.

There are numerous possibilities for rigging a jury rudder, including making full use of a wind-vane steering system with its attendant servo or auxiliary rudder, and organising drogues to pull to one side or the other, but the most commonly effective method is to press the spinnaker pole or booming-out pole into service.

THE SPINNAKER POLE RUDDER

This system has repeatedly proved its worth. The pole itself may not have enough water resistance to function well, but it generally works adequately if something larger, such as a dinghy paddle or a floorboard, is secured to its outboard end.

The pole is passed out through the pushpit and attached to its piping with a lashing which allows universal movement. The steering oar thus formed is easy enough to understand, but one or two problems seem to recur in practice:

- One of these is to keep the business end below the surface against the tendency of the water flow to float the pole up. This can be neutralised in some cases by adding weights – the anchor, for instance – to the end, which offers the added advantage of increasing the pole's water resistance.
- The second difficulty is that steering by hand in this way can rapidly exhaust the helmsman. The favourite answer is to rig control lines through quarter blocks and

lead them to the sheet winches. It sometimes takes two to steer, but the results are usually satisfactory.

MAN OVERBOARD

Man overboard recovery is a two-phase operation. First, the boat must be stopped close to any casualties for long enough to be able to secure them, and secondly it must stay there for long enough for the crew to assist them back on board.

MAINTAINING CONTACT WITH THE CASUALTY

Whatever else happens during the execution of the operation, it is vital that contact with the casualty is never lost. Someone on board should be watching the whole time. This may be a designated watcher in a fully crewed boat, or it might have to be the helmsman in a short-handed cruiser. In the dark, the job can prove impossible if unassisted.

Traditionally, help takes the form of floating strobes deployed from the stern of the boat the instant somebody falls over. Today, personal radio beacons are available at reasonable cost which can and do save lives. Personal EPIRBs (emergency position indicating radio beacons), carried by watch keepers and activated automatically should they hit the water, alert the international search and rescue (SAR) authorities.

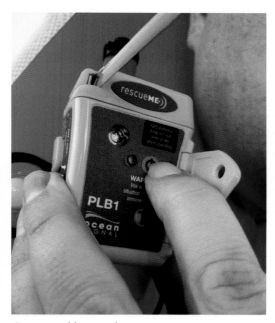

A personal locator beacon

If casualties are wearing lifejackets and you cannot find them, they are thus in with a chance of rescue in due course, albeit not a great one. An arguably better arrangement using today's technology is to equip the watch with a personal AIS transponder. This puts out a signal picked up by the yacht's VHF radio and sent direct to the chart plotter.

A light, in particular a hand-held flare carried in the oilskin pocket, can be invaluable for maintaining contact

The casualty shows up on the chart screen, complete with range and bearing, and the yacht can be steered directly to them. A recovery can then be made in relatively short order, rather than a lone swimmer quietly suffering increasing hypothermia while remote SAR crews are scrambled.

Lifebuoy and light stowed ready to throw

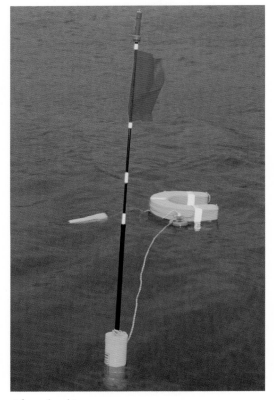

After chucking

ELECTRONIC NAVIGATION SYSTEMS' 'MOB' FUNCTION

Most good quality electronic chart plotters carry a 'man-overboard' (MOB) button to be pressed when needed. This marks the vessel's current position with what is effectively a new waypoint. Bearing and distance to the position when the button was pressed are available, as is the pictorial view.

These functions can be of inestimable benefit in finding a lost person in the water, particularly in the dark, but it should never be forgotten that the position given is a terrestrial position and relates to the global grid. If there is tide or current on the move, the casualty and the boat will both be gliding away from the position at the same rate and in the same direction. I have yet to find a plotter that offers to make corrections for this very real factor.

To put into perspective the errors which can accrue, a two-knot tide will drift the victim 200 metres from his original position in as little as three minutes. After fifteen minutes, he will be half a mile away. The advantages of a personal AIS beacon showing the casualty's real-time position are emphasised by this stark fact.

RETURNING TO THE CASUALTY

While never forgetting the essential necessity to remain in touch, there are a number of systems for bringing a boat to rest close by, or even alongside, a crew member in the water. Which you opt for will depend on your boat, the conditions, and your assessment of your own competence. Here are three of the most effective methods, but whichever you select on the day, remember that it is better to stop 5 yards from a conscious casualty still in reasonable condition and toss a line rather than to risk injury by coming alongside in a seaway.

It should go without saying that while sailing schools teach these manoeuvres, exercises are generally carried out in benign conditions. When running Yachtmaster Instructor assessment courses, I used to do them in wind against tide off the Needles Lighthouse in pitch darkness. That concentrated the mind on how things may be in heavy weather. What you do about this is up to you.

THE CRASH STOP & REACH-TURN-REACH

The crash stop system keeps you initially close to the casualty. Following it up with the reach-turn-reach delivers the best chance of rescue, given a boat that is easy to sail and whose engine has been disabled. In a modern cruiser with a mainsheet arrangement that sees the sheet rigged forward of the cockpit on the coachroof, requiring a winch to sheet it in, this may not be the case. Regardless of whether or not the engine works, or what the arrangements for sheeting the mainsail may be, the crash stop is generally the first action in any overboard situation under sail.

THE CRASH STOP

As soon as casualty hits the water under sail, the first action is to crash stop the boat.

1. Tack, regardless of your point of sailing, bringing the boat through the wind. Do not release the headsail sheet, thus leaving the jib aback.
2. In theory this will heave her to. In practice it can be a messy business with bights of mainsheet looping round spare winches or unaware crewmen, but sometimes it works beautifully.
3. The boat may now drift close enough to the victim for you to pass him a floating line. If she doesn't make it, you can

sometimes persuade her by juggling sheets and tiller or applying a little help from the engine after first ensuring no ropes are in the water. If you simply cannot get anywhere near him, at least you are making little way through the water other than your drift, so you can reassure him, lob him some buoyant safety gear and / or a light, then decide which other method to bring into action. 'Crash Stop' is therefore a good starting point on the spur of the moment.

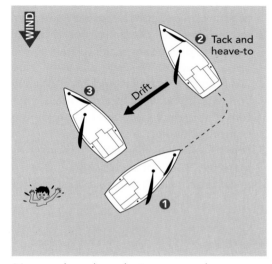

Man overboard: crash stop approach

REACH-TURN-REACH

Again under sail, some say that this is the best of all the systems, but it has two serious drawbacks in certain cases: boat handling of a high standard is required, and the technique involves sailing some distance away from the casualty while working up the sea room for the pick-up approach. At night, especially if you are not certain that the victim has caught hold of the light you threw, or if the light has failed as the older type often does, the risk of losing touch in the dark may be too great.

Notwithstanding these more-than-reasonable criticisms, practising this method will not be time wasted, particularly if you suffer from an unreliable engine or one that will not deliver adequate punch to manoeuvre in heavy seas. What is more if, in spite of all precautions, you wrap up your propeller, there may well be little alternative. You have more sail control on a 'reach-turn-reach' than any other approach.

Here is a step-by-step breakdown of the whole manoeuvre:

1. From the crash-stop position as you drift away from the casualty, throw over the liferings, dan-buoys, Jonbuoys or lights as appropriate, and designate a watcher.

2. Immediately sail the boat away, properly trimmed, on a beam reach relative to the apparent wind. This will place the true wind abaft the beam and should leave you where you want to be to make your turn. If it is dark, note your approximate compass heading.

3. When you've enough room to manoeuvre, either tack or gybe. Bear in mind that tacking will take you further upwind. Gybing will lose you ground. Either may be what you want. You'll hear experts saying, 'Never gybe in an emergency situation,' but like most absolutes, such a statement may prove inappropriate at sea. Gybing a 32ft masthead sloop single-handed in a force 6 should present no problems at all to a competent adult and might, or might not be, the best course of action. Executing the same manoeuvre in a 40ft gaff cutter with two sets of running backstays would be a non-starter.

4. Having made your turn, steer the boat towards the casualty. If you cannot see him or the safety gear, come onto a reciprocal compass heading and look out dead ahead.

5. As soon as you have the boat headed for the casualty, let all your sheets right off and note whether or not the sails can spill wind. If they do and the boat is positioned upwind of what would be a close-hauled heading to the casualty,

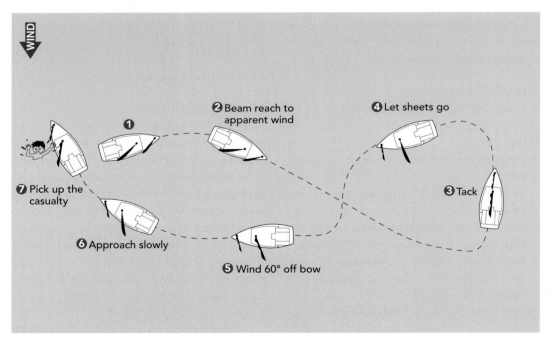

Man overboard: reach-turn-reach approach

you are probably on a close reach.

6. Now check your masthead wind indicator to see whether the wind is around 60° off the bow as it should be. The close reach allows perfect speed control because you can ease your sheets to slow down or pull them in to speed up. If your reach is too broad you will not be able to spill the mainsail because the boom will bring up against the shrouds while the leech of the sail is still full. If you are too far to leeward, the casualty will be in your boat's windward `no-go zone'. If you are rather broader off than you would like, but feel you are still in with a chance, it may be possible to further de-power the mainsail by letting off the kicking strap or vang, a technique that is notably effective with fractional rigs.

7. If the boat is successfully on a close reach, lose way and slowly approach the casualty. If she is `below' a reach (i.e. to leeward of the desired heading, or too hard on the wind), make up what ground you can close-hauled, 'above' the target, before bearing away and spilling wind on your final, close-reaching approach. If you don't achieve this in good time, the boat will stall into the no-go zone as soon as you try to slow down, leaving no choice but to tack up to the victim.

When you find yourself 'above' the desired heading (you'll know this because you won't be able to persuade the mainsail to spill wind properly), you must bear away sharply, run downwind for a few seconds, then steer once more for the casualty while re-assessing your angle to the wind.

The reason why you sailed so far away on the initial beam reach was in order to have enough sea room to execute either of these last two manoeuvres if they should be required. Do not waste that ground through indecision.

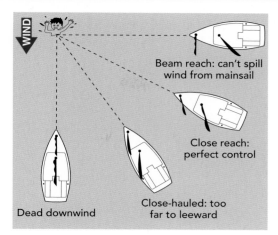

The close reach approach

Beam reach: can't spill wind from mainsail

Close reach: perfect control

Close-hauled: too far to leeward

Dead downwind

THE MOTOR-SAILING METHOD

While some hold strong views that the job of manoeuvring to a swimmer is better tackled under sail alone because there can be no danger of injuring him with the propeller, the motor-sailing method will remain the hot favourite for skippers with honest doubts about their capacity to sail accurately in close quarters in a gale of wind. Plenty of us may fall into that category of honest mariners. Also, motor-sailing is also the only realistic hope your inexperienced crew may have to handle the boat in the event of the ultimate horror of going overboard yourself.

1. First, crash-stop the boat as described above, deploying floating gear as appropriate.

2. Then, watching the victim's position at all times, roll away the headsail.

3. Allow the boat to run downwind of the casualty and then start the engine after first making absolutely sure that no rope of any description can end up anywhere near the propeller.

4. The final approach is made from downwind with the mainsail loosely sheeted amidships. The sail will steady the boat and the engine will supply the required control. Unless the wind and

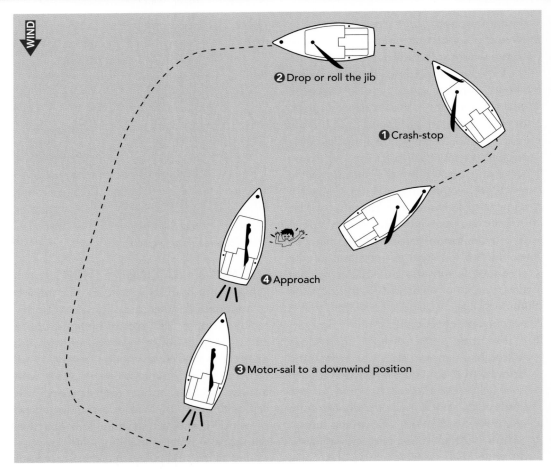

WIND

❷ Drop or roll the jib

❶ Crash-stop

❹ Approach

❸ Motor-sail to a downwind position

Man overboard: motor-sailing approach

waves are of such magnitude that there is inadequate power to prevail against them, motor-sailing will generally produce the desired result, even if it is less tidy than some theorists would like to see. Never forget, though, that you have a propeller thrashing around down there which can inflict shocking injuries on a swimmer.

THE PICK-UP

Wherever sailing instructors gather together the question of whether to pick up on the windward or leeward side is mooted. Consensus is rarely reached. The reason is that, like so many facets of seafaring, it all depends upon the circumstance.

On the face of things, the **leeward pick-up** looks like the favourite. If you stop to windward of the casualty with the breeze well out on your weather bow, the stalling boat will slide down towards them, particularly if you steer up towards the wind to luff off the last of her way. You will then be able to pick up amidships, but watch out for the flogging jibsheet. If you've a roller genoa, furl it before you go out on the deck. In a strong wind it will often pay to roll it away before your final approach.

If this sounds an ideal scenario, it is important to understand that, should you choose to pick up the casualty on your leeward side, you may drift down onto them causing distress, further injury or worse. Also, to place the boat where you want her you will usually have to turn during the final approach, passing the casualty under the bows, which is no joke for them even if you get it right.

On the other hand, if you try to circumvent these real difficulties in a big blow by picking up on the **windward side**, it is more than likely that you will make so much leeway as you slow down that you won't get close enough even to heave a line. You must therefore try both methods yourself on a windy day. Do it out in the waves, not in sheltered water, and use a dummy of some sort that makes no leeway like a real swimmer, or at least a fender tied to a bucket, to see what happens. Then you'll have a chance of choosing the best of two evils on the day when it matters.

Don't forget that while much that is written about such pickups assumes the casualty is unconscious or at least unable to self-help, this is more often not the case. If the person in the water is able, don't try to come alongside. Aim instead for a point five metres or so away and toss them a line.

If you lose someone while you are running with a preventer on or a spinnaker set, the coolest deck work will be needed if the victim is not to disappear from view, possibly for ever, while you are sorting out the gear. Work out in your mind what you would do if this were to happen, then try it and make sure your plan is feasible, whichever is your preferred pick-up drill.

Because of the danger of losing contact, it is vital to steer a straight course while sorting out the gear, and to note what it is. You can then return on the reciprocal, under power if necessary, and have a fair chance of finding them.

This sort of contingency underlines the good sense of using an AIS transponder, so that the casualty is never lost to the instruments' view.

HELPING THE CASUALTY TO BOARD THE YACHT

When the casualty is alongside, the next task is to hoist him aboard. There are cases of fit people clambering straight back up to the deck without any assistance other than that of a shipmate giving them a leg up. With modern high-freeboard yachts this is becoming more far-fetched, and anybody who is not in fine shape will stand no chance.

In other circumstances, the best way when the person in the water is still compos mentis and retains some body strength is to try the boarding ladder if you have one. However, should this be permanently rigged on the transom, you may find that in a seaway its pounding up and down generates danger, threatening to stab or brain the person it is supposed to be saving. This can be ameliorated by laying the boat beam-on to the seas so she rolls rather than pitches. A sufficiently robust ladder that can be lowered well into the sea from the beam is likely to be of more use, but most such boarding ladders sold commercially are too short for this.

I can personally testify to the fact that, in the absence of a boarding ladder, success can sometimes be achieved by lowering a bight of line into the water. The tail of the jibsheet is perfect for the job. The swimmer steps into this and, as the boat rolls, he raises himself up as best he can while helpers on deck take up the slack around a cockpit winch. After two or three 'grunts' he will probably be high enough to roll under the top guardrail. The lower rail should be let go in order to make the job easier, which can only be done if the guardrails are secured and tensioned with lanyards rather than rigging screws. Even a large person fully kitted up in oilskins and the rest can generally slither under the upper wire, and it is a hundred times easier to do that than to try clambering over it.

If this does not work, or the casualty is too weak even to attempt it, you will have to devise a lifting arrangement using a halyard, a tuning block and a winch and / or a tackle.

Pass a rope around the casualty's shoulders under the arms, for securing them to the vessel. If there's a harness in use, so much the better. Attach the lower block of a tackle (a dedicated one is best, pre-measured, stowed in stops and ready for this purpose) to the harness, and the upper block to a spare halyard, the spinnaker halyard being the most useful where one is fitted. The tackle is now stretched out using the halyard and the tail of the tackle is led, via a suitable turning block, to a primary sheet winch. The casualty can now be raised or helped up by

the weakest person on board. The power of a 4:1 tackle backed up by even a modest winch will lift almost anyone, however wet.

Received wisdom is that lifting by a sling under the arms is a bad idea. It can and certainly does sometimes cause secondary symptoms after recovery that may prove fatal. The alternative is to contrive a means of lifting the casualty horizontally. Slings can be purchased that help us to do this, but deploying anything simpler than I have already suggested in a ten-foot sea in 40 knots of wind in the dark, may not be realistic. The skipper must make the judgement call.

It must be understood that the above recommendations are merely suggestions. On some boats they may work under certain circumstances, but on others they may appear useless fantasies. It is therefore vital that all crews discuss and experiment with various methods of lifting a heavy weight (two large water carriers, for example) out of the sea.

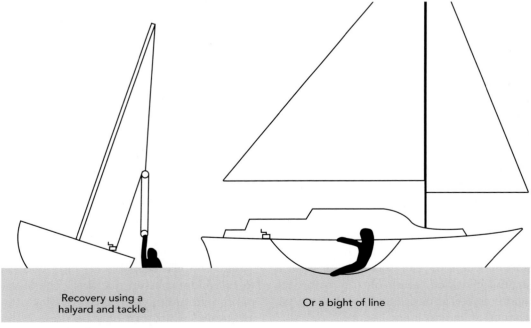

Recovery using a
halyard and tackle

Or a bight of line

Two methods of recovery

SEARCH & RESCUE

If the yacht is within relatively easy reach of Search and Rescue centres, which would cover most continental coastal waters, there is a strong argument recommending that the first thing to do on shouting 'man-overboard' is to fire-up the VHF and put out a MAYDAY, or at least activate the red general emergency button on a DSC set. The SAR people are very happy for you to do this, saying they would rather answer a dozen calls for assistance where the casualty has been recovered by the time they arrive than turn up ten minutes too late in the one case where the skipper was slow about making a call.

The practical reality seems to be that if you are on a yacht with a large crew, it makes sense to detail one of them to call for assistance while you are taking your own steps to recover the person in the water. If you are short-handed and have just had your effective crew reduced by a half or a third, it would seem more sensible at least to try to recover the victim yourself before quitting the deck, possibly losing sight of the casualty as a result, in order to call rescuers who may be some time in arriving.

If you have serious doubts about your ability to recover the casualty unassisted, there is no doubt that you must call immediately.

FLOODING

While flooding is not specifically a hazard of heavy weather, it is perhaps more likely when the boat is being thrown about than otherwise. For example, a cockpit locker lid may burst open during a modest knockdown and take a serious amount of water which will certainly end up in the bilge. There are times when companionway washboards or doors must be removed to allow folks to move in and out. I've personally experienced a wall of water almost up to my knees while enthroned on the forward head because the yacht was pooped at the wrong moment. Added to such dramatic contingencies must be the ever-present possibility of skin fitting or general plumbing failure.

In the first type of case, everyone can see where the water has come from, and few will need encouraging to pump or bucket it out. It's more insidious and a great deal more alarming to see the water level in the bilge rising and have no clue about where it's coming from. This is where some pre-planning comes in.

It might be unrealistic to suggest what follows is going to be a popular diversion during an afternoon jaunt in the sunshine, but if a long passage is planned, it makes sense that the bilge, the skin fittings and associated piping are divided up by the number of able crew members.

Each person's duty is to learn about his or her section and, in the event of serious flooding, to inspect that part of the yacht that they know best. Such an arrangement is far more likely to produce a quick solution than leaving everything to the skipper as the only person with any real idea of where everything is.

In an ideal world, each skin fitting has a wooden bung attached loosely close to it. If it fails, all that is needed is the lump hammer because the bung to block the hole is all ready to go. If this isn't going to happen, at least be sure all hands know where the bungs are and that there is a plentiful variety.

11

THE LIFERAFT –
THE FINAL RESORT

The liferaft and its canister

Typical contents of a liferaft

Throughout this book we have emphasised the importance of self-reliance. However, the time may arrive when even the most prudent preparations and tactics are brought to nothing by the unexpected. Often, this comes about by stress of bad weather and results in a decision to abandon ship. In the final chapter we shall discuss when you should consider taking this most drastic of steps but, first, it is important that any skipper fully appreciates what is being asked of a crew who leave the yacht and take to the liferaft.

Years of evaluated experience, beginning with the catastrophic 1979 Fastnet Race, have indicated that a liferaft is a second-rate survival option compared to a floating yacht not irremediably on fire. There are a sizeable number of cases where a crew, fearing for their safety, have boarded the liferaft with one or more losing their lives as a direct result, while the still-buoyant yacht was towed safely into port after the storm died down.

Such incidents speak for themselves, and the conclusion is inescapable. A Search and Rescue team will see a yacht, even a dismasted one, long before a tiny liferaft shows up among the waves. Furthermore, boarding a raft is sometimes dangerous, as is being rescued from it. Survival rations, including water, that can be stowed inside the raft are inevitably limited, while the yacht herself is often at least partially victualled; and unless she is waterlogged, the chances of staying warm and dry are far better aboard her than in a tiny raft surrounded by water.

The message is crystal clear. Except in case of fire, do not step off the yacht unless sinking is irreversible and imminent.

But, since this book is about being prepared, I will take you through the procedures if you do have to launch the liferaft. It is a good idea to go on a Sea Survival Course to familiarise yourself with the procedures, such as the one we photographed run by First Class Sailing.

ACTIONS BEFORE BOARDING THE RAFT

- **Warmth**: Have all hands put on extra clothing, full oilskins, lifejackets and harnesses. Keep dry if at all possible.
- **Water**: Insist that your crew drink as much water as they can hold. Not only will this raise body fluid levels and help prevent early dehydration, it will also discourage the problem of urine retention which may otherwise beset some of them in the tight social confines of the raft. Fill extra water containers to load into the raft.
- **Food**: If there is time, eat sugar /

carbohydrate foods such as biscuits or chocolate bars in preference to fats or proteins. Take as much of this into the raft as you can if there is a chance.
- **MAYDAY**: Continue broadcasting MAYDAY messages to augment a DSC call until the last possible moment. This also goes for communicating by radio with a rescue vessel or service.

> ### MAYDAY
>
> A 'Mayday' distress message is a formal affair and should be sent out in this manner, speaking slowly and calmly:
> - MAYDAY MAYDAY MAYDAY
> - THIS IS YACHT LEAD BALLOON, LEAD BALLOON, LEAD BALLOON
> - MAYDAY LEAD BALLOON
> - MY POSITION IS: LAT/LONG (FROM GPS), OR RANGE & BEARING FROM CHARTED OBJECT
> - NATURE OF DISTRESS & ASSISTANCE REQUIRED
> - NUMBER OF PERSONS ABOARD
> - ANY OTHER USEFUL INFORMATION (ROCKETS FIRED, ETC.)
> - 'OVER'
>
> Wait for a response, then reply accordingly & keep calm.

LAUNCHING THE RAFT

- **Painter**: Whether the raft is stowed in a canister on deck or a valise elsewhere, make sure that the painter is secured to a strong point on board the yacht prior to launching. There is at least 30ft of line inside the liferaft pack, so do not be dismayed if it feels 'unattached' to the raft itself. When you have checked that all is properly secured, check again.

- **Launch**: Remove the lashings and check the water is clear of all obstructions. Then heave the canister / valise over the side of the yacht. The lee side is generally preferable. (If the boat is on fire, choose a site as far from the blaze as possible.)

- **Inflate**: Pull on the painter until it is all out of the pack. At the end, give a sharp, positive tug. There will be a sound like a small explosion and the raft will self-inflate, bursting out of the case as it does

Attach the painter to a strong point

Remove lashings, check water for obstructions, check the painter again & launch the liferaft to leeward (if there is a fire, choose a site far from the blaze)

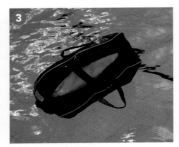

The liferaft should hit the water clear of the boat

Pull the painter, which may be up to 10 metres long to bring the liferaft in your lee

A small explosion indicates that the raft is starting to inflate

It soon bursts out of its case ...

... inflating itself

... and folding out

Finally, the canopy inflates

so. The process may take up to 30 seconds. Note that the inflation valves regulate the gas pressure in the tubes. Depending on ambient temperature the gas inflation cylinder may deliver more gas than required. Any excess is exhausted through the valves, making a noise like a child deflating a balloon. This is perfectly in order and no cause for alarm. The canopy inflates last.

- **Prepare to Board**: The painter is usually attached to the raft near the door. If possible, pull the raft right up alongside the yacht.

BOARDING THE RAFT

Keep dry if you possibly can, and board a strong person first, so that he or she can help weaker crew members in the event of problems. He / she should go to the windward side to help stabilise the raft, then be ready to give assistance.

If this means the skipper is first aboard, then so be it.

They are then followed by other crew members. Make sure nobody has any sharp objects projecting from their gear before they board. Once aboard slip your arms through the grab lines and hold on.

Enter the raft dry if possible, putting a strong person on board first

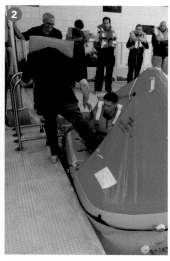

This will help stabilise the raft

Assistance can be offered to others as they board

Once on board, spread out around the perimeter of the raft, slip your arms through the grab lines and hold on

Don't forget to take extra water, victuals, some plastic bags, first-aid kit, sleeping bags, etc. that you have time to load up. Also, a waterproof grab bag for the EPIRB, flares, hand-held VHF, mobile phone and, if you have one, a portable charger. A good book can also be an important aid to morale maintenance.

OPERATING IN THE WATER

ENTERING THE WATER

In certain circumstances you may not be able to enter the liferaft dry – for example, if the liferaft has capsized or is impossible to bring alongside.

If you have to enter the water fully kitted up, remember to hold your nose, hold down your lifejacket and keep your feet together. Never dive. Always go feet first

In the water in high winds and seas, actively protect your airways and use the lifejacket hood if one is fitted

If you are in the water for a long time, huddle together as a group to prevent heat loss and maintain morale

If you need to move, form a chain and move together

RIGHTING A CAPSIZED RAFT

Occasionally, a raft will inflate upside down, or blow over before its water ballast chambers have filled. This is bad news because at least one person will have to climb into the water to right it, but at least the righting process is likely to be successful, so things could be much worse.

The most suitable individual, who will usually be the best swimmer, inflates their lifejacket and climbs onto the up-turned raft in the vicinity of the gas bottle. They stand on this, grip the righting strap or boarding ladder and lean backwards, ideally into the wind. The raft will flop over on top of the swimmer, who then works out from underneath, orienting if necessary using the ladder or strap. There is no cause for alarm as the world goes temporarily dark, because the lifejacket will buoy the head up into its own air space under the raft floor.

Approach the raft where the gas bottle is, feet first on your back. Put your feet on the side of the raft and pull on the webbing strap

The liferaft will slowly come up ...

... and up

... and over

BOARDING A RAFT WHICH HAS DRIFTED AWAY ON ITS PAINTER

Sometimes, in very high winds or waves, it may prove impossible to bring the inflated raft alongside, even by leading the painter to a winch. You will then have to board by entering the water. If this is your unfortunate lot, send the strongest person first. He should inflate his lifejacket, clip his harness to the painter, swim to the raft and scramble aboard. The rest of the crew then follow suit. It is vital to clip on, or people may drift away and be lost.

A good deal of water will enter the raft with the people – possibly knee deep. Bail this out as soon as possible – it is a deadly danger as it can spoil stores and even drown people in the dark in a crowded raft.

As soon as everyone has boarded, go into the 'Cut, Stream, Close, Maintain' routine (see below), but make special emphasis on drying if possible and keeping warm at all costs.

Arrive at the raft in your chain

Send the strongest on board first, boarding using the ladder …

… then scrambling into the raft

Others can then be assisted aboard

Once two are aboard, others can be assisted by lifting them from under their arms

This can help with weaker people

BOARDING WITH A CASUALTY

If you need to leave the liferaft to retrieve a casualty, protect your airway and keep hold of the raft as you enter the water. Secure yourself to the raft with the floating line supplied. If the casualty is further away than this, think very hard before letting go.

Swim the casualty to the raft

Have at least two of the crew in the raft to help assist the casualty on board, leaving someone in the water so the casualty is not alone

Grab the casualty under the arms ...

... and lift up

Pull backwards ...

... safely into the raft

RAFT CAPSIZING DURING BOARDING

On capsizing, the survivors quit the raft, keeping in touch with both it and one another. The team leader rights the raft as described earlier. The survivors then re-board and start bailing.

Don't panic under the raft. Remember these rules and all will be well. Once the full crew are aboard, the raft is unlikely to capsize again, but if it does and stays upside down, you are safe because it will float high. Evacuate the raft in an orderly manner, stay together and in touch with the raft (tied on preferably), right the raft as described above, then re-board it.

ON BOARD THE RAFT

Boarding the liferaft is only the beginning. You have not survived until you have been rescued. What you do immediately you climb into your raft may materially affect your chances. The following four headings, which should be learnt, are the beginning of a chance of life:

- **Cut**: As soon as everybody is aboard, and assuming that sinking or total conflagration is imminent, cut the painter with the clearly marked safety knife you should find stowed near the entrance to the raft. In heavy weather the raft will be carried rapidly to leeward.
- **Stream**: When the liferaft is well clear of the yacht and any wreckage, stream the drogue. This serves a number of purposes. Not only does the drogue diminish drift, it also maintains the raft in an attitude that keeps its door away from direct wind and wave assault. Thirdly, it fulfils an important function in maintaining raft stability. If the original drogue is lost, you will find a spare in the raft's gear. Secure it to a strong point such as the painter loop, then stream it.
- **Close**: Unless the weather takes a turn

for the better, close the door of the raft using slip knots (bows) on the tapes. If the floor is inflatable, deal with this now, then have everybody sit round the edges of the raft, for maximum stability. If heat builds up, as it may do, do not hesitate to 'crack' the door from time to time, so long as wave ingress is not a problem.

- **Maintain**: Dry off the liferaft floor, check it for leaks and plug these as necessary with the rubber bungs provided. Now is the time to take stock of your situation, appoint a leader if necessary, quantify your survival equipment and make sure your EPIRB (Emergency Position Indicating Radio Beacon) is activated if appropriate.

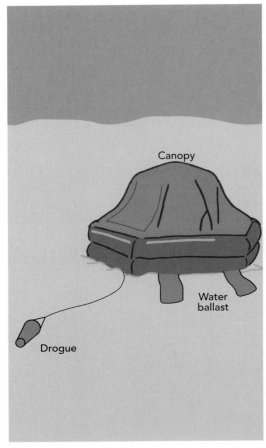

Canopy

Water ballast

Drogue

The liferaft in action

Only go for the liferaft as a last resort

SECONDARY ACTIONS ON BOARD THE RAFT

Once the initial actions (Cut, Stream, Close, Maintain) have been affected, life goes on. Before settling into a long-term routine, the following items are worth dealing with.

- **Roll call**: If you have a large crew, make sure everyone is aboard the raft. If any are missing, look out for them, call and be ready to throw the quoit and floating line to pull them in.

- **Seasickness**: This is a real problem in rafts because the motion is so extreme. As any dedicated sufferer can tell you, ultimately this common ailment can erode a person's will to survive. It is therefore imperative to issue all hands with seasickness pills as soon as possible, 'whether they need them or not'. If people are being sick and cannot reach the entrance, they should be issued with plastic bags. Vomit washing around the floor of a liferaft does nothing to build morale.

- **Injuries**: Do what you can at this stage. Your raft pack contains a basic kit with instructions if you haven't managed to load more comprehensive equipment.
- **Bailing**: Keep mopping up the floor.
- **Body warmth**: Remember, this is vital. If people are cold and shivering, encourage them to huddle up, but look out for problems associated with loss of stability. If you have Thermal Protective Aids – modern rafts with SOLAS (Safety of Life at Sea) kits have two – give them to those most in need. They consist of large plastic bags for live bodies.
- **Routine and watches**: Organise a rota for look-out, whose duties include keeping a weather eye open via the door for rescue craft, passing shipping or aircraft.
- **Use of VHF radio**: The hand-held radio should be used for MAYDAY messages on a sensible, regular basis. Bear in mind that battery conservation is crucial.
- **Pyrotechnics**: Flares will be found in the raft pack, but you should bring any left from the yacht as well, if at all possible. Use red rockets as advised in the next chapter ('Outside Assistance') and save pin-point reds for when rescuers are in sight.

- **Ventilation**: The raft should be vented by the watch every half-hour or so. A sleep-inducing CO_2 build-up may result from failure to deal with this.
- **Passing water**: Encourage everyone to urinate after a couple of hours, not only for comfort's sake, but also to avoid problems which may accompany urine retention. Do not worry if urine is dark and smoky after a day or more in the raft. This is normal.
- **Rations**: Do not issue anything for the first 24 hours, except to children and the injured. Children suffer greater fluid heat loss than adults and this should be born constantly in mind. If you foresee a protracted spell in the raft, issue rations at set times, such as sunrise, noon and sunset.
- **Morale**: The skipper should issue rations fairly, maintain confidence in eventual rescue and do everything possible to keep the crew cheerful and determined to survive. The situation and the elements combine to sap the will to live; this tendency must be actively fought.

Always bear in mind that the rescue operation, when it arrives, may prove extremely hazardous. The crew may be severely weakened by their ordeal, so the skipper's job is not finished until each person is safely aboard the rescue vehicle, whether it be helicopter, merchant ship or lifeboat.

ACTIONS WHEN RESCUE IS IN SIGHT

This involves flares, hand-held VHF, personal AIS transmitters or any other means of attracting attention. Details are given in the next chapter.

If a full crew are to be lifted by hi-line transfer, they will have to move out from beneath the canopy. If rescue is absolutely certain – and only then – some current thinking is that you should have all hands come out one by one and sit around the tubes of the raft, deflating the canopy as seems sensible.

12
OUTSIDE ASSISTANCE

Search and Rescue (SAR) personnel take great satisfaction in their work. They are highly trained people who are generally operating the finest equipment that technology can provide. They prefer to be in action rather than to be training or otherwise waiting to use their skills, and they have all chosen to be there. They understand better than most people that nobody is infallible and that there will always be unforeseeable circumstances which will cause even the best organised outfits to require assistance.

Bearing these facts in mind, you will see that to call for help need not be a cause for shame or create a crisis of conscience over putting other peoples' lives at risk. Certainly, there are cases of lifeboats being lost with all hands, but such incidents are mercifully exceedingly rare. The SAR services would much prefer you to call them in good time than to leave matters until they are too late. After all, the helicopter can always return to base, and the lifeboat crew can go home. No harm will be done if you sort out your own problems while they are on their way.

CALLING OUTSIDE ASSISTANCE

THE PAN PAN CALL

The vast majority of yachtsmen and women do their sailing within easy reach of SAR help. If this applies to you and you see a situation developing that you fear might cause you to require help at a later time, send out a PAN PAN (urgency) call. This will enable the Coastguard to alert the SAR who may then stand by until either they are needed or you confirm that you have managed to deal with the problem.

A typical example would be loss of steering in heavy weather. You might sensibly choose to call the Coastguard, tell them your position, the nature of your trouble and what you are doing about it. If your efforts come to nothing and real personal danger ensues, you can upgrade to MAYDAY, but if you succeed with your emergency tiller, you can advise accordingly and stand down the PAN PAN.

If one of your crew is injured, perhaps by being thrown across the saloon, and you are concerned but do not feel an emergency lift is needed, use a PAN PAN MEDICO call. The Coastguard will then hook you up for a free consultation with a doctor, after which you can decide with more confidence what action is to be taken.

CALLING FOR IMMEDIATE ASSISTANCE – MAYDAY BROADCAST

The great question here for most people is, 'Do I or Don't I?' The answer is very simple. One of Britain's most famous lifeboat cox'ns once remarked to me that, 'If you think you might need rescuing, you do need rescuing.' Circumstances that may be fine for one individual might be far too much for someone else to cope with. Danger can be a subjective thing.

If you need help and you have a two-way radio, send out a MAYDAY call (see Chapter 11). The Coastguard will probably respond, but if they are out of range a ship or another yacht may come back and relay your message on. Once communication has been established, things become self-explanatory.

If you have no working radio, you will have to use flares (see below) or utilise one of the various means of attracting assistance detailed in all commercial nautical almanacs.

PYROTECHNICS

Always have one set of up-to-date flares on board. Official advice is to hand in your old ones for destruction, but, at your own risk, there is another point of view. If you have space to carry them and unless they are obviously in poor condition, any pyrotechnic device recently past its expiry

date has a fair chance of firing successfully. Even flares that look as if they came from Noah's Ark have been known to work 'on the night', so whether you hang onto them against a time when it may be a case of 'the more the merrier', is a question of risk assessment. Thank goodness that in the UK at least, such decisions are left up to the individual. In France, it is illegal to carry out of date flares.

RED ROCKET PARACHUTE FLARES

These are for attracting the attention of people who do not know you are there. Whatever numbers you carry, you are unlikely to have as many as you would like, so use them sparingly. A good time to use a couple might be when a ship's lights are in clear view, ideally showing a bows-on aspect, or perhaps when you are within visual range of an inhabited shore.

Use your rockets in pairs. The psychology is simple. Somebody may notice your first one, perhaps just as it is dying, and doesn't really believe it. They may have glimpsed it out of the comer of an eye and, after all, you don't come across red flares every day. Nonetheless, they look for another just to be sure they saw nothing. When your second goes up, it grabs their attention and keeps it.

Red rocket parachute flares

Fire rockets at an angle slightly down from the vertical and facing to leeward. They re-curve to windward and should explode overhead.

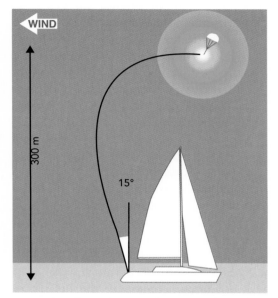

Point the flare downwind: A parachute flare seeks the wind and ends up overhead before the parachute opens

RED HAND-HELD (PINPOINT) FLARES

Hold these to leeward of you and your boat or raft. If you can see a vessel's sidelights, she can see your flare because, although you are low down in the waves, your light is 100 times brighter than hers. Its purpose is to pinpoint your position.

Red hand-held flares

SMOKE FLARES

These are now usually of the floating canister type, though you may still come across a hand-held example. They are deployed to leeward of you and show your whereabouts in daylight by the abundance of orange smoke they generate. They are particularly useful when a helicopter is looking to identify a casualty among a lot of boats.

Smoke flares

WHITE FLARES

White rockets are not part of your 'official' flare pack, but it is well worth carrying one or two in order to light up the world if ever you need to. Man Overboard is a case in point. The white hand-held flare is used to indicate your position when you require no assistance. I saved my ship and my life with one of these in a winter storm halfway across the Bay of Biscay. Make sure you have a couple even though you may only need them once in a lifetime.

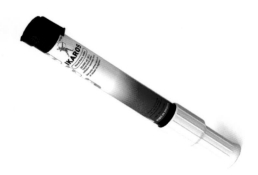

White flares

HELICOPTER RESCUE

Helicopters cannot stay up forever. They run low on fuel, so always be aware that where they are concerned, there is not a moment to be lost.

When you are expecting a helicopter, you will probably know the direction from which it will arrive. Look out for it and when you see it in the distance, do all you can to attract its attention. Use VHF to indicate your relative position from it ('45° on your port bow', etc.), show pin-point flares, but never fire a rocket in the vicinity of a helicopter. Helicopters are massively noisy and it is not always easy to follow the pilot's VHF transmissions. Don't be afraid to ask him to repeat his messages.

PREPARING THE BOAT FOR HELICOPTER RESCUE

- Because the pilot is on the aircraft's starboard bow, he can see into your cockpit from the port quarter. This is where the winchman will land when he comes aboard if you are still under command, so take down all projections from aft such as aerials, ensign staffs and even topping lifts. Lower the main boom

if this is appropriate to make boarding as easy as you can.

- Stand by to be briefed via VHF. You will probably be asked to motor to windward at your best speed or, if you have no engine, to sail close-hauled on port tack. Be prepared for bright searchlights at night and stand by with your deck lights. You may be surveyed for what seems ages before anything happens. The downdraft from the rotors is not so bad as you fear it may be, but the noise is awesome.

- Once given a course and speed, stick to it whatever happens. Choose a reliable helmsman and leave him or her to steer until the last minute comes to take them off the boat as well.

- If conditions are desperate and the yacht is not under command, the helicopter pilot may decide to tell you to climb into the dinghy or liferaft for pick-up. In less extreme circumstances, or in the case of a medical emergency to be lifted off, he will probably opt for a Hi-line transfer. This works well under most circumstances and has been generally favoured for many years.

HI-LINE TRANSFER

The essence of this technique is that the helicopter lowers a light line to the yacht. The line is attached to the winchman as he is lowered, enabling the yacht's crew to pull him aboard as he lands.

Here is the sequence of events:

■ The hi-line is lowered towards you. It has a heavy weight on the end to stabilise it (1).

■ In theory you should let the hi-line touch the sea to dump static electricity, but this does not always happen.

■ When you have the line in hand, take up the slack, flaking it down. Never make the hi-line fast (2). In the event of snagging and becoming entangled with your gear, a 'weak link' will break.

■ The helicopter may now move off so the pilot can take another look. Keep working the slack on the line.

■ When the pilot is satisfied with his position, the winchman is lowered.

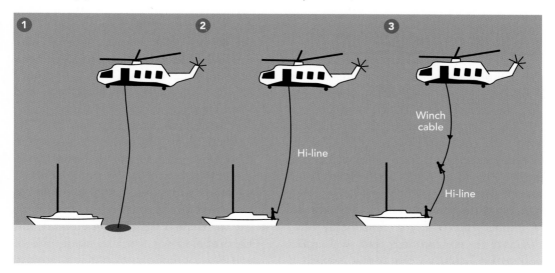

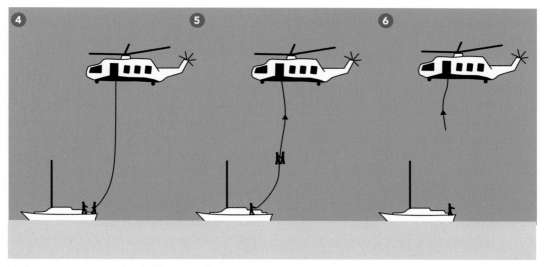

Helicopter rescue with a hi-line transfer

Occasionally there will be no person on the wire, only a strop or a stretcher. Use the hi-line to guide him or it aboard. Be ready for a hefty pull if required (3).

- If a winchman comes aboard, he will take charge of the rescue (4), so follow his instructions. If not, secure evacuees sensibly and signal to the helicopter's crew to lift them with a vigorous 'thumbs up'. Slide the toggle on the strop as close to the body as possible and encourage evacuees to keep their arms down by their sides.
- Ease the hi-line as the lift is in progress. If necessary, use it to stop any swinging about (5).
- Release the hi-line when you are told to do so (6).

Note that in a real emergency, you may receive two strops at once for two people to be lifted at a time.

LIFEBOAT RESCUE

WAITING FOR THE LIFEBOAT

Once the Coastguard or other rescue co-ordinator tells you the lifeboat is on its way, you have a number of things to attend to.

The first priority is to talk on the VHF with the cox'n if possible. This serves several purposes, but an unexpected one is that your tone of voice offers him some insight into your state of mind. A quiet, capable statement will tell him you are still in control but that you reasonably have decided to ask for help. He will expect you to be useful in the rescue, which is preferable for everybody. If your voice is clearly agitated, he will realise that your judgement may be taking a beating, so he knows what to expect. However you are feeling, communicate.

- Give your position by the best means available. A GPS position is favoured. It's a good idea to tell the cox'n how you have determined the position you give him.
- Tell the cox'n about your boat, the nature of your distress, what you are doing about it, and what you'd like the lifeboat to do.
- If a tow seems a possibility, take what steps you can to prepare for it. Back up your bow cleats or bollards by cranking them back with lines to the primary winches, thus spreading the load. Look out some chafing gear, etc.
- Kit up your crew in lifejackets and harnesses.
- You may see the lifeboat with its flashing blue light before it sees you. If so, describe your relative position to the cox'n. If you have no radio contact, be ready with pinpoint flares or smoke canisters.
- Do not shine a light at the lifeboat, but be prepared for them to shine one at you. Try not to look straight at it, despite the temptation.

The lifeboat will have fenders which the cox'n may choose to use, but you must be ready for structural damage if the lifeboat comes alongside in heavy weather. The best thing you can do for yourself if you are not going to abandon your boat is to use well-stuffed sailbags as fenders. They work satisfactorily for brief periods. Deployed for long, of course, their contents will be damaged.

Do not try to instigate the transfer of crew unless the lifeboat people ask you to, and remember that you remain in command of your own vessel even though you would be wise to follow the cox'n's advice.

HELPING OTHERS AT SEA

Should you sight a red flare or any other distress signal, or hear a MAYDAY, you are obliged to go to assist. If you hear no acknowledgement of the MAYDAY message or a PAN PAN message, you should instigate MAYDAY RELAY procedure and respond yourself if appropriate.

Once in a while, you may find yourself the first vessel to arrive when someone else is in distress. You are then officially designated the 'On-Scene Commander'. In addition to your normal concern for the safety of other seafarers, you will now take on certain duties:

- Make clear your intentions to anyone who calls on Channel 16.
- Do anything you can to help the distressed vessel.
- You remain On-Scene Commander until a larger or better-equipped vessel arrives. This could be a commercial or military ship, an SAR helicopter or a lifeboat.
- If you are in the vicinity of a rescue but not actually involved, stand well off and monitor events on Channel 16.

Never forget that if it is you in trouble, whatever the nature of your distress or whoever is coming to your assistance, keep calm, continue communicating and do whatever you can to help those who are helping you. Above all, believe that you are going to survive.

Running down to the Bishop Rock out of the North Atlantic. All hands smiling as the sun comes out and the wind drops from gale force. They'll have some tales to tell ...

PHOTO CREDITS

All photographs © Tom Cunliffe except:
Alastair Buchan (from *Short-Handed Sailing*): P32 (bottom left), 106
Ben Sutcliffe Marine: P34 (right)
E P Barrus: P113
Fernhurst Books (from *The New Crew's Pocketbook*): P46 (right), P47 (right), P48 (top)
Fernhurst Books / Sealand Photography (from *West Country Cruising Companion*): P23
Heather Guppy: P27 (bottom left), P28
Hydrovane International Marine Inc.: P116
iStock: P22 (Mgodden)
Jeremy Atkins: P26 (bottom left, top right, bottom right), P27 (top left), P32 (right), P45, P46 (bottom left), P47 (left), P128, P129, P130, P131, P132, P133
MCA: P140
Nicola Rodriguez (from *Sail Away*): P118 (top)
Ocean Safety: P117, P126, P138, P139
Pat Manley (from *Diesels Afloat*): P36 (left & right), P114
Performance Rigging: P110
Peter Firstbrook (from *Coastwise*): P20 (bottom)
PPL: P112 (Australian Maritime Safety Authority/PPL), P135 (RAAF/PPL)
Shutterstock: P19 (Oskari Porkka – left), P19 (Maximillian cabinet – right), P24 (Gill Copeland), P26 (Ian_Stewart – top left), P31 (Insect World – bottom left), P37 (Benedek Alpar), P96 (Martin Augustus)

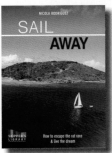

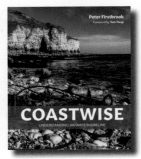